GOLF LESSONS FROM THE PROS

GOLF LESSONS FROM THE PROS

Compiled by the editors

of SPORTS

ILLUSTRATED

illustrated by **Anthony Ravielli**

Prentice-Hall, Inc.

Englewood Cliffs, N.J.

Portions of this book were previously published in *Tips from the Top*,
Book I, copyright 1955 by Time, Inc., and *Tips from the Top*,
Book II, copyright 1956 by Time, Inc.

PREFACE

There are many authenticated stories from tournament golf about seasoned players who have suddenly improved their play immensely by accepting a simple but vital tip. A number of years ago Ben Hogan and amateur Don Cherry, the singing golfer, were playing together in a tournament. Cherry was having a terrible time. For three or four holes Hogan watched in his typical tight-lipped fashion while Cherry wildly hooked one shot after another, barely keeping the ball on the golf course. After Cherry reappeared from the trees and rough on a particularly frustrating hole even the uncommunicative Hogan could keep his peace no longer.

"You say you're from Texas?" Hogan asked Cherry, his voice heavy with skepticism.

"Yes," said Cherry, "Wichita Falls."

"Well, damn," said Hogan, who comes from Ft. Worth, "then move your right hand over on top of the shaft and start hitting the ball straight like a Texan." Cherry immediately made the correction and has been hitting the ball straight ever since. In 1953 and '55 he was named to the Walker Cup team. Last summer, though he is an amateur who now plays infrequently, he finished in a tie for ninth with Hogan in the U.S. Open.

Without doubt two of the best-known and most picturesque tips in the vast repertory of golf instruction came from two of the game's most picturesque personalities. The late Babe Zaharias, an uninhibited conversationalist, once passed on this bit of advice to the constantly growing population of women golfers: "Loosen up your girdle and swing away." On another occasion Sam Snead was equally forthright: while playing a round with Dwight D. Eisenhower at the Greenbrier, the President asked for Sam's opinion of his game. "It's fine except for just one thing," Snead answered. "You should stick your fanny out a little more, Mr. President."

These two items of instruction are more colorful than most,

but they make a point about what we have tried to achieve with GOLF LESSONS FROM THE PROS, and what SPORTS ILLUS-TRATED magazine has achieved in its series, TIPS FROM THE TOP, from which the lessons in this book are drawn. From the beginning, the idea behind TIPS FROM THE TOP was to present a frequent instructional item that would supply golfers with a brief, practical, precise, expert, interesting and easily understood tip. To guarantee that the tips would be authoritative, the editors enlisted the assistance, not only of the best known playing profes-sionals, but also of many club professionals—men and women who played very little tournament golf, but whose skill as teach-ers was well known and respected in golfing circles. Each pro contributed two tips that he considered valuable, either because they had proved to be very successful teaching aids or because they had worked for him under tournament pressure. The maga-zine had the good fortune to obtain the services of artist Anthony Ravielli to illustrate each tip. Ravielli is singularly endowed for this kind of work. Not only is he a genuine lover of golf, but he has written and illustrated an excellent book on anatomy. The first TIP FROM THE TOP, Gene Sarazen on the "After-Forty Finger" (chapter 96 of this book), appeared in the December 20, 1954 issue, and the tips have been appearing more or less regu-larly since.

This collection is the third to be published in hard-cover book form and it is by far the largest. It includes some outstanding tips selected from the two previous volumes, plus over seventy tips never before presented in book form. Because the collection is so large the lessons have been grouped into five classifications: *The Grip and the Stance, The Fundamentals of the Swing, Hit-ting the Ball from Tee to Green, Getting Out of Trouble,* and *On and Around the Green.* This makes it possible for each reader to go directly to the area of his greatest weakness, the one he is obviously most interested in improving. If he is one who has trouble chipping or putting, for instance, he will probably find a number of tips in Part V, *On and Around the Green,* that can help immediately. Anyone frightened (and who isn't?) at the prospect of having to dig his ball out of a sand trap should read Part IV, *Getting Out of Trouble.* Even good drivers may find Lionel Hebert's tip on "Driving Tight Fairways," a useful one for an everlastingly difficult problem in golf.

Table of Contents

Part I
The Grip and the Stance

CLAUDE HARMON

Masters Champion, 1948

Checking the Grip with the Club Head

I never play a shot without first glancing at my hands. What I check before address is the alignment of the grip with the face of the club. They go together.

Most golfers know of this relationship between the hands and the club face—at least, they know it theoretically—but the ordinary golfer rarely puts it into practice. Very often, while he is fiddling with his grip, he inadvertently rotates the shaft and twists the club face out of alignment. Most pros, on the other hand, knowing that the grip is correct only when it is correctly aligned with the club face, take pains to check this fundamental of good golf. If you have ever watched Jimmy Demaret, you have no doubt seen him affix his grip, raising the club until his hands are only a foot or so in front of his eyes. Then Jimmy sights down the shaft and checks both his hands and the club head as one unit.

Gripping a club, you see, is like aiming a rifle. If your hands are improperly aligned with the club head, you will hit only a few isolated accurate shots. I never trust my grip entirely to feel. It can go off too easily, and after a couple of days the incorrect grip will feel fine and natural. Once you start your swing, you must trust entirely to feel, for your eye is fixed on the ball. However, before you start to play your shot, you have the chance to check the relation of the grip and the club head visually. The results are well worth the effort.

2

Addressing the ball, Harmon checks grip and club head

Correct alignment

Exaggerated depiction of incorrect alignment

BILL GORDON

Tam O'Shanter Golf Club, Niles, Ill.

The Friendly Grip

A good golfer is recognized by his grip. Rightly so, for a proper grip is the basis for at least 60% of a man's swing. Beginners, and players who are uncertain of their game, tend to grab the club and hang on like grim death, or else they hold the shaft gingerly as if they were afraid of the damage they might inflict on the ball. Both excesses can throw you off your game. Whenever I see a pupil's fingernails whitening as he holds the club, I ask him to let go for a minute and shake hands with me. Usually he gives me a nice firm "friendly" grip, and that's just what I want—not a bone-crusher or a limp paw. Once we've shaken hands, I ask him to grip his golf club the same way, firmly but in a friendly way. His execution of shots usually improves.

I always check to see that my pupils' hands are set properly on the shaft—that goes without saying—but what I am trying to bring out here is the importance of gripping with the right amount of pressure. To the beginner, the golf grip feels at first like the most unnatural thing in the world, but he will soon find out that only through practicing the correct grip can he control with any degree of steadiness the arc of the club and the flight of the ball. Repetition of the right grip will result, in due course, in confidence and a well-founded swing that will bring good results regularly. Give the friendly grip a try.

Bill Gordon demonstrates (top) how the left hand grips the club firmly, but not rigidly. The right hand is about to "shake hands" with the shaft in a similarly friendly grip. The proper grip will give you (below) the correct, controlled hand action

FAY CROCKER

Club de Golf, Montevideo, Uruguay

Welding the Grip

I have had one theory about golf ever since I was knee high to a duck: nature, with golfers in mind, shaped the right palm so that the left thumb fits into it perfectly. When the left thumb and the thumb pad of the right hand are welded together, the golfer's hands will stay together and work as one, and nothing is more fundamentally important than this.

Women golfers frequently want to know why they are hitting the ball straight but are getting no distance at all. Their trouble frequently is that their grip comes apart. Much more often than men, women will open their hands at the top of the backswing. They tend to do this because their forearms are not as strong as a man's. The constructive move, in any event, is to make sure that the left thumb and the right palm are in perfect contact with each other throughout the swing—and especially at the top of the backswing. If you have a genuinely welded grip, then, even if you are late with your footwork or some other aspect of the synchronized action of a fine golf swing, you will still produce a fairly good golf shot. What is more, keeping the two hands firmly together is the direct route not only to consistency but also to power.

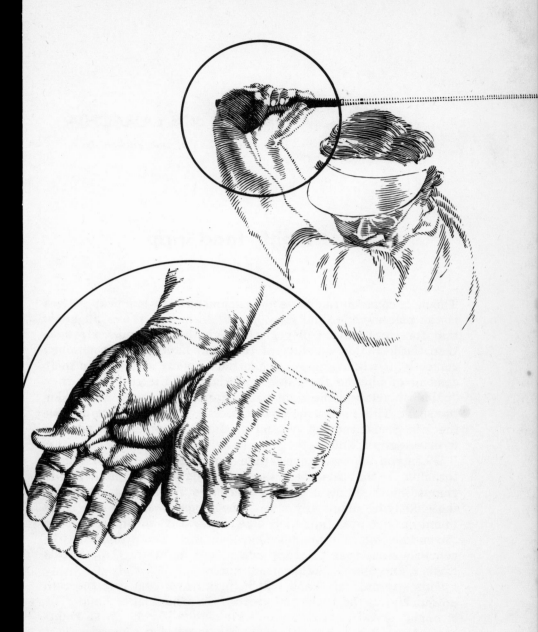

The left thumb fits perfectly into
the thumb pad of the right hand.
This welds the hands together

7

JOE LAMACHIA

Locust Hill Country Club, Pittsford, N. Y.

The Right-Hand Grip

The most common fault I've noticed among high-handicap golfers is the placement of the right hand on the shaft. We all know that for right-handed players the right hand is much stronger than the left. Consequently, if the right hand is not positioned correctly, it will overpower the left. Too many golfers ruin their chances of playing the game well right off the reel when they "palm" the club in the right hand, tipping that hand well under the shaft. This makes the strong hand even stronger, wipes out the left almost completely, and produces a tremendous number of errors of all kinds.

When you take your overlapping grip, affix the right hand on the club so that the shaft does not lodge in the palm but is gripped by the fingers. (If you opened your hand, you would see the club lying diagonally across the fingers.) As for the right thumb, fold it over to the left side of the shaft so that it touches the middle finger and the forefinger—lightly. Almost immediately you will sense that the right hand feels different, that it feels weaker, and that the left feels stronger.

This stronger left hand will help you avoid picking the club up quickly on the backswing with a dominant right hand. The stronger left will not only stop your tendency to be an all-right-handed golfer but will also allow you to develop a more correct over-all swing pattern. And then you have a chance to improve.

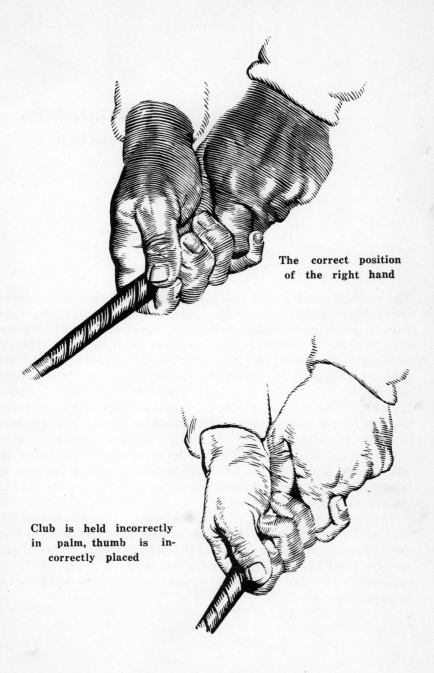

The correct position
of the right hand

Club is held incorrectly
in palm, thumb is in-
correctly placed

9

GRAHAM ROSS

Dallas Athletic Club Country Club, Dallas, Texas

The Left-Hand Grip

The balance and feel of a golf club are transmitted to the player through the hands. Few golfers understand as clearly as they should which parts of the palm and fingers do the actual gripping. To put it another way, they remain hazy about which muscles of the hand hold the club, exert the pressure, and, by their position and action, initiate the golf swing and influence its execution.

In regard to the left hand's grip on the shaft, I should like to propose that a golfer think for a minute about the way he picks up a pitcher of water. The last three fingers of your hand grip the handle of the pitcher. They're the ones that lift and hold it. The thumb and index finger, however, are relaxed—you could hold a pencil or a golf ball between them and your grip on the pitcher wouldn't be affected.

That is how you should grip the golf club with the left hand. The last three fingers provide the power to lift and swing the club; they remain glued to the shaft. The thumb and index finger are applied to the shaft much more lightly. They provide as little or as much pressure as is necessary on those shots in which touch is important.

10

Graham Ross illustrates
the correct left-hand grip

GEORGE CORCORAN

Greensboro CC, N. C.

The Modified Baseball Grip

The woman golfer too frequently thinks in terms of trying to steer the ball with her hands. When she tries to do that, the tendency is to pull the club head across the ball (from the outside in), and a slice is the result.

To overcome this, I recommend that women golfers—and beginners especially—use what I call a modified baseball grip. The left thumb is in line down the shaft of the club, as in orthodox golf grips, but there is no interlocking or overlapping with the little finger of the right hand. This grip causes a golfer to get more right hand into her action. More right hand will enable her to get more power into her swing, and it keeps her from pulling the club head across the ball, makes her swing through the ball and straightens out that slice. This modified baseball grip may result in a slight hook—which would be good for most women golfers. (This is the reverse of what is true of most men; they tend to overemphasize the hit, to get too much right hand into their swings.)

I also think that the woman golfer should wear a full-fingered glove on her left hand. It gives her a much better grip than she could get with her bare hand or a half-fingered glove.

George Corcoran advises a modified
baseball grip for women golfers

WILLIE KLEIN

Gripping with the Palm

A bad grip has wrecked many a golf game. It can cause hooks and slices and increase the natural tendency of most golfers to use their right arm in too strong a fashion. I advocate gripping the club in the palm of the left hand, not the fingers. If you get all of the grip from the fingers, it increases the chances of letting your wrist bend. A lot of golfers tend to let their right hand slip around toward the bottom of the shaft because it makes the arm feel stronger. That's the thing you should be trying to get away from—that feeling of power in the right arm. If the right arm slips toward the bottom of the shaft, it leads you to pick the club up drastically on the backswing. The result is you smother the ball. Some golfers start off with a correct right-hand grip but they don't maintain this correct grip throughout the backswing. This causes the golfer to close the face of his club as it reaches the ball, and a hook results.

Turning to the left hand: this is where the slice begins. Gripping the club too much in the fingers makes the wrist collapse on the backswing. This opens the club face and a slice results.

A rule of thumb works something like this: If you're slicing, look at your left hand and see if the wrist is collapsing. If you're hooking, reappraise your right-hand grip.

14

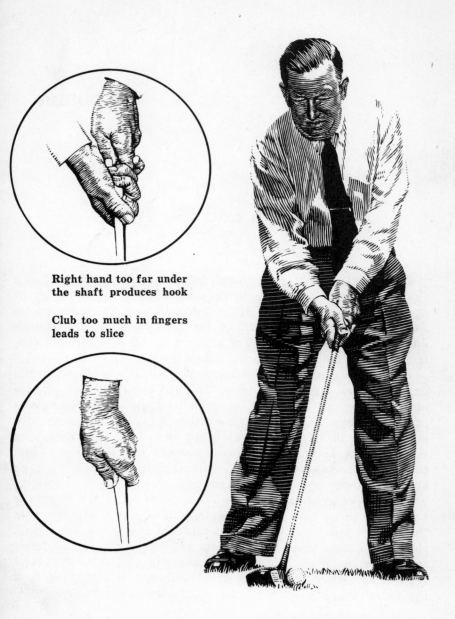

Right hand too far under
the shaft produces hook

Club too much in fingers
leads to slice

Willie Klein's correct grip

15

ED DUDLEY

The Grip and the Swing

As paradoxical as it may sound, relaxed, well-played golf is a "pressure game"! Pressure, as properly applied by the fingers as they grip the club shaft, is in my opinion one of the fundamental factors underlying good golf. In fact, the position of the hands on the club is the principal key to control, and only through control can a golfer rise above the dub stage.

How much pressure? How applied? Well, the pressure should be that amount that provides a "feel" of the club without producing tenseness. It should be applied by the last three fingers of the left hand. Or, to put it another way, the hands are not supposed to be limp on the club but in a position where they feel ready to do their work: to act as the swivel of the swing, to control the takeaway as the club starts on its backswing, to start the downmove on the downswing.

The proper grip—meaning that the pressure of the fingers is right as well as the position they occupy on the shaft—permits the all-important cocking of the wrists at the top of the swing, eliminating tenseness in the wrists and forearms. It also tends to produce a straight but not unnaturally stiff left arm. It is worth your while to get this grip fundamental right, for it is the foundation on which all the other actions are built.

The correct movements on the backswing and the downswing
can be executed only if the hands are properly on the club

KATHY CORNELIUS
Miami Valley Golf Club, Dayton, Ohio

Gripping for a Controlled Hook

Women can get more distance off the tee—10 to 15 more yards—by making a small alteration of the left-hand grip. The conventional grip for men calls for the left thumb to be set down the middle of the shaft, with the V pointing to the chin. The grip change for women which I advocate consists of turning the left hand farther to the right. The thumb rides down the side of the shaft and the V points to your right shoulder.

Women are not as strong as men, and we can't fly the ball as far in the air simply by applying arm and hand power. Getting out a good distance means getting as much roll as possible on the tee-shot. This slight alteration of the grip gives you this added roll, for your hands come into the ball in such a way as to impart right-to-left draw to the shot—a slight, controlled hook. Most women have good timing and I think it will take the majority of them very little time to adjust to this changed grip and the different hitting action.

In this general connection, let me add that the spot in the swing where most women lose their power is at the top of the backswing. They let the left wrist sag and break down, toward the ground. Regardless of what grip you use, be sure you keep the left hand strong and keep it under the shaft at the top of the backswing.

**Keep left hand strong
at top of swing**

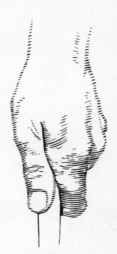

**Conventional
left-hand grip**

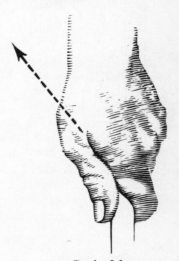

**Revised for
greater distance**

HARRY COOPER

Metropolis Country Club, White Plains, N. Y.

Spotting the Ball

There's been a decided trend of late toward playing all shots (from the wedge right down to the wooden clubs) with the ball spotted in just about the same position with reference to its distance between the left and right heels. For pro stars who can practice eight hours a day, this ultra-uniformism works out all right. They are able to acquire great feel and to compensate with their hand action for the slight differences between the contact point of one club and another. But this method is very harmful for the average golfer. If you don't move the ball, you must indeed change your hand action a bit for every different club, and this is well beyond the average golfer's ability. Uniform spotting gets him into all sorts of trouble.

It is much more sensible to graduate the position of the ball to fit the varying physical properties of each club—playing the key club, the five-iron, in the center of the stance and moving the ball back about an eighth of a turn as the loft of the club increases, an eighth of a turn forward as the loft decreases. In this way you accomplish your adjustment immediately, and there is no need to compensate with your hand action when you execute your swing.

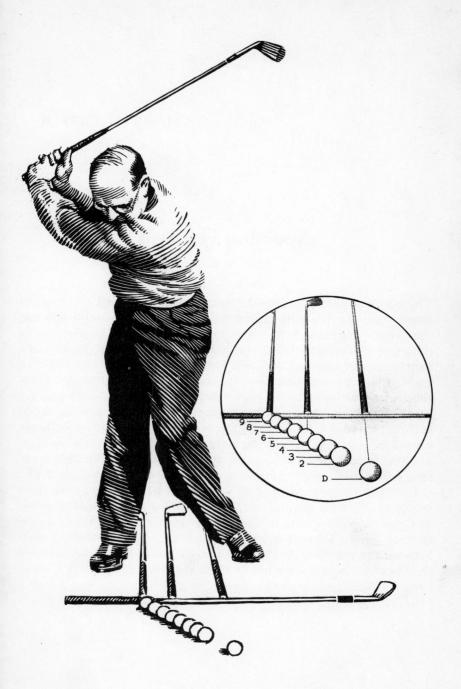

II

ED OLIVER

Denver, Colo.

Avoiding Flatness

The major problem for chunky men in golf is keeping their swing from being too flat—that is, on too shallow or horizontal a plane. The first thing they must learn in order to avoid this flatness is to take a more restricted pivot. Employing a slightly open stance helps considerably to cut down an excessive body turn. So does concentrating on taking the club back on a straight line from the ball, since it leads the player into a more upright swing. As the illustration shows, I recommend that when heavily built golfers practice, they place a club parallel to the line of flight as a visual aid to coming back straight on the line.

I am strictly a hands-player myself. But even for the average golfer of chunky physique I advocate the short, upright swing with the emphasis on firmness and timing. Don't let your left arm get stiff at address. Make sure your shoulders come underneath your chin, not out and around your chin. As for stances, I have found I get the best results by playing the woods with an open stance, the medium irons from a square stance, and the short irons from a slightly open stance.

Stance for medium irons

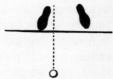

For short irons

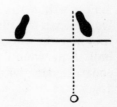

For woods

23

12

CLAUDE HARMON

Masters Champion, 1948

Lining Up the Club Face

As a rule, golfers don't pay enough attention to the face of the club. The face of the golf club is so small that few golfers realize how important it is in correct shot-making for that face to be square to the ball throughout the swing.

A surprisingly large number of golfers don't even start their swing with the face square. They think they do, but somewhere these golfers have picked up the erroneous notion that it is the top line of the club face that one should refer to to determine if the face is square at address—that is, resting so that it is perpendicular to the intended line of flight. Now, that's not right. It's the bottom line of the face that determines whether the club is square or not.

One other thought on this matter. If the player rushes his backswing, the club will change position in his hands. It's bound to—just the way a pitcher in baseball would lose control of the ball if he wound up like lightning. You must start square and control your swing so that you stay square.

Correct: bottom of club face
square to line of flight

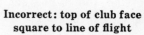

Incorrect: top of club face
square to line of flight

13

LOUISE SUGGS

Sea Island, Ga.

Lining Up the Shot

One fundamental fault that I have observed to be shared by many women golfers is that they start with their hands behind the ball at address and, consequently, have their hands in a weak position throughout their swing.

The error begins when a player lines up faultily. In the process of lining up her hands with the club face and also with the target, a golfer tends to get her hands behind the club face in the act of placing the club behind the ball to sight the line. After obtaining her line, she forgets to get her hands back in front of the club face. Having the hands in front is more important than is generally understood. It sets up a strong left side, with the left hand the leader at all times. It leads to a more natural cock of the wrists on the backswing and a more natural body turn. With the hands behind, the right hand is in a position to take charge, thus introducing many errors. The golfer will pull the club too far inside or pick it up too sharply, and will generally fall into a strained incorrect position at the top and into a lurching approach to impact.

When you are getting the hands set at address, that is the time to extend the left arm comfortably. You won't overswing, but you will be in a fully extended position at the top.

Incorrect: hands behind

Correct: hands ahead

27

14

MIKE TURNESA

Knollwood Country Club, White Plains, N. Y.

The Relaxed Address

A number of golfers I know who want to improve their game handicap their progress at the very beginning of the stroke. When they address the ball, they stretch their arms out so tautly that their forearms become as stiff as boards and their shoulders are all knotted up. Before they even begin the swing, they are extremely tense—and you cannot be muscularly rigid and expect to play good golf.

When you are addressing the ball, your arms should be comfortably flexed, not extended rigidly. Now there are many ways to obtain this position. One method which I personally find helpful is to address the ball slightly off the toe of the club. During the swing, the arms are bound to do some stretching, for they extend themselves naturally. This stretching brings the center of the club head squarely into the ball. It is not a conscious effort to "reach for the ball." You simply arrive at the ball, your arms fully extended as they should be, but muscularly alive.

A large number of our finest players, Bob Jones and Tommy Armour, for example, employed this method of address. They found it suited them. It may not suit everyone, but I seriously recommend it to the beginner and the "hacker" as a tip they should examine. It can be a sound provision for relaxation throughout the swing.

Tense address of many golfers

The relaxed address, ball at toe of club

15

JIM BROWNING

Weston Golf Club, Weston, Mass.

The Elbows at Address

One of the most common swing-wrecking faults of the high-handicap golfer is his tendency to pick the club up at the start of the backswing. The moment he makes that faulty move, the golfer has virtually surrendered all chances of playing a good shot. His hands and his arms are just where they shouldn't be, and they remain hopelessly wrong throughout the remainder of the backswing and the downswing. He usually cannot help chopping at the ball. In his muscular entanglement, it is the only course of action open to him.

The idea, of course, is to *swing* the club back. If you do, the odds are that you will then swing down and through the shot correctly. I have one tip for starting the backswing properly that has worked wonders with my pupils. I instruct them to push their elbows closer together just before they start to take the club back. When you do this, you will find it is almost impossible to pick the club up. Furthermore, it helps you to take the club back in a smooth sweeping arc. I might add that among the pros—Ben Hogan is perhaps the most obvious exponent—this habit of pushing their elbows toward each other is almost second nature.

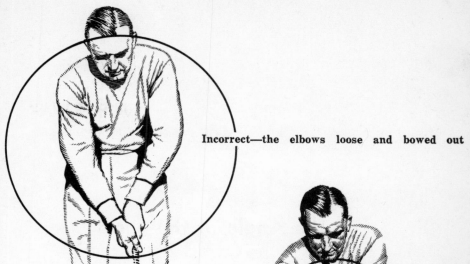

Incorrect—the elbows loose and bowed out

Correct—the elbows pushed together at address

16

JOE NOVAK

Bel Air Country Club, Beverly Hills, Calif.

The Angle of the Shaft

In golf, all the power generated by the body action must reach the club through the action of the hands. Many beginners fail to get the left hand placed properly and comfortably on the club. In this regard, they would do well to consider the construction of the club itself. All golf clubs are built with what can be termed a "hooked-in face"—that is, the face, the part of the club head which meets the ball, is not built truly parallel to the line of the shaft but is hooked in, as illustrated in the diagrams on the opposite page.

Consequently, if a golfer aligns himself so that the shaft is square to the line of flight, the face of his club will actually be pointed to the left of the desired line. Furthermore, his left hand, by being too much in front of the club, is in a weakened position for the entire stroke.

In order to correct these faults, the golfer should tilt the shaft forward—place his hands so that they ride slightly ahead of the club head, not behind it. The left hand then assumes a strong and natural position. Simultaneously, the face of the club is then poised absolutely square to the line of flight. Some beginners hesitate to adopt this alignment for fear of slicing but, actually, the incorrect position encourages slicing and the correct position does not.

(Below) Diagram A, the hooked face of the golf club; Diagram B, with shaft at right angle to line of flight, club head faces to left of line

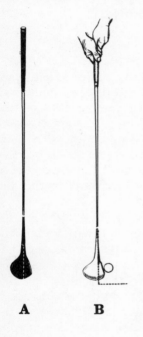

A   B

Correct position, shaft tilted forward to bring the club face perpendicular to line of flight

33

Part II
The Fundamentals of the Swing

17

GARDNER DICKINSON, JR.

North Palm Beach, Fla.

Active Legwork

If you are constructed like George Bayer—the last time I looked, George stood six-feet-five and weighed around 240—and if you are strong and well-coordinated to boot, whipping the club through the ball at a tremendous speed calls for no extraordinary measures. You simply swing and it happens. On the other hand, slim fellows of medium height like myself (who are outweighed almost two to one by the likes of George) really have to work at developing club-head speed.

Footwork is what will do it for the player of slim build, and that is what I give the balance of my practice time to—developing the action with my feet and legs that will make up for lack of brawn. On the backswing, in order to prevent any swaying and in order to store up maximum energy to release later, I push forward, to the inside, on the instep of my right foot. This helps you harness your power, but you must be sure you don't overdo it and tip forward with your trunk. Then, on the downswing, it helps me to increase my club-head acceleration, I find, if I push forward with my right knee—push it toward my left knee—as I am coming into the ball. Plenty of practice is required before this kind of footwork even begins to become second nature. But the added club-head speed produces added yardage that is more than worth all the hours you spend lowering the practice tees.

On backswing, Dickinson pushes forward on right instep

On downswing, Dickinson pushes forward with right knee

18

SAM SNEAD

Masters Champion, 1949, 1952 and 1954

The Importance of Relaxed Legs

Being tense ruins more golf shots for more players than any other thing. When a golfer is all tightened up, he doesn't have a chance to swing correctly at the ball. These unrelaxed golfers figure that the faster they swing the more distance they'll get, and you've seen hundreds of them who go back as fast as they come down. They're the boys who have inspired that popular hustler's slogan: "Give me a man with a fast backswing and a fat wallet."

Rhythm and timing are the most important things in a golf swing. You can't get them—you can't even come close to getting them—unless you're relaxed; and I mean relaxed not only in the arms and hands but throughout the body, especially through the legs. Walter Hagen used to say that as long as he could keep his legs relaxed he didn't worry. The rest would take care of itself. I agree with him one hundred per cent. When your legs and ankles are nice and supple, only then will your muscles be able to do the work you want them to do. Only then can you pivot right and get that sense of rhythm that helps you to go back in one piece and to start down from the top with everything moving in close harmony.

The golfer with tensed
legs cannot pivot

The tied-up golfer is
necessarily off balance
through the ball

Relaxation leads to the desired actions

19

WALLY GRANT

Mt. Lebanon Golf Club, Pittsburgh

Forward Weight Shift

The so-called exchange of weight—to the right side when swinging back and the reverse shift to the left side before starting the club down—is widely misunderstood by golfers today. Certainly the top players do not *feel* the exchange of weight in the way it is expressed to beginners or to average golfers trying to improve.

My thoughts on the matter are that you should pay much less attention than is commonly done to the left-to-right shift going back and concentrate on the forward shift to the left side which is a dynamic part of the proper swing. Now, on this forward shift of weight, if the golfer thinks of initiating it from *right to left,* working from the feet to the hips—as he does when he throws a baseball overhand—he will develop a free rhythmic swing of the club. The left knee will become a major factor in executing this forward move correctly. All tournament players seem to rock the left knee to the right while taking the club back and then rock it laterally ahead of the ball before starting the club down. Actually, the left knee is still bent slightly until after the ball is struck and doesn't straighten until the swing is completed.

Remember also in this forward shift that you start the weight forward lightly and not in one abrupt movement, letting it gather gently as the swing progresses.

**Wally Grant demonstrates start
of right-to-left shift of weight**

20

JACKIE PUNG

Honolulu

The Lateral Move

One of the drabbest but most important elements in improving your golf game is learning to exchange your weight. Everyone knows the fundamentals. On the backswing, your weight—not all of it but most of it—moves to the right. Then on the downswing you transfer your weight back to the left side as you move into and through the ball. The point I want to bring out ties in with the fact that your body doesn't remain stationary on the same axis as you perform the backswing and then the downswing. You must be certain you move into the ball as you play the shot, and only through practice do you learn how to move sufficiently laterally from right to left.

All this, as I have said, is as dull as dishwater compared to the more charming aspects of the golf swing. It has to be learned, though, and to bring a little pleasure to it I follow a practice exercise that has a little fun as well as worth attached to it. With the sun at my back, I take two golf clubs and place one on the ground on each side of my shadow. During my swing I want my shadow to stay within the confines set up by these two clubs. At the top of the backswing, I can see how much room I have to fill in coming forward to have my shadow finish at the left stick.

Not moving forward is a common fault among women golfers and explains why they don't hit the ball as solidly and as well as they should. With the golf club guides women can do a lot, I think, to overcome the bad habit of getting stuck on the right side. It also helps to correct a bad tendency to lean forward as you hit into the shot.

42

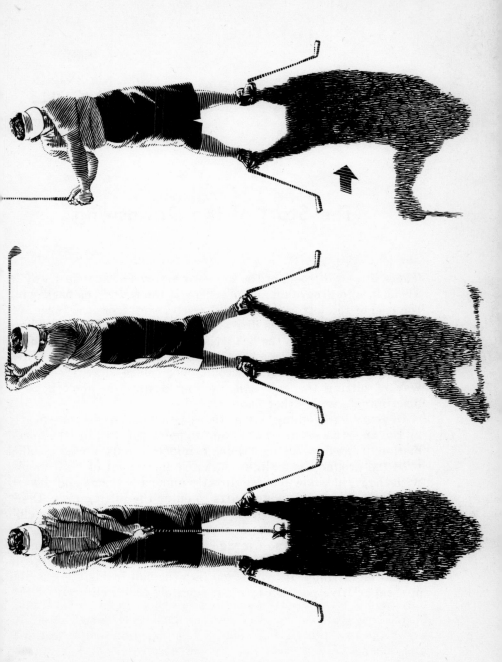

21

BERT NICOLLS

Belmont CC, Mass.

The Start of the Downswing

There is a lot of room at the top—for error. The soundest way to avoid it is to groove an action where at the top of the backswing the heel of the left hand points directly away from the target or, to say it another way, is directly behind the line of flight. There should be no crease in the left wrist. The beauty of this position is twofold. First, you don't have to be an extraordinarily talented player to execute this. And second, once you're there, it's a great way of hitting the golf ball: coming down, you don't have to discriminate with either hand.

In regard to coming down, there is a little move that nearly all the fine strikers use that I want to point out. Ideally, the initial motion of the downswing (which brings the shaft almost parallel with the ground) is a slight clockwise movement of both hands, with the right elbow moving directly under the hands and toward the right hip as the swing starts to enter the hitting area. Don't think for a minute that this is an easy thing to do right. The club seems too far behind you, and your hands are all eagerness to hit. This is not for the average golfer. But for the very good players, this finesse move at the hardest point in the swing is worth the learning. It brings you into the ball inside the line and in a superlative position to hit it squarely and accurately.

The heel of the left hand is
directly behind line of flight

The finesse position coming down

45

22

JOE KNESPER

Mayfield CC, Lyndhurst, Ohio

How to Cure Hitting from the Top

Most errors in golf are caused by hitting from the top and coming into the ball from outside the line. Proper coiling and uncoiling will prevent this. Most average golfers, however, don't have a clear picture in their minds as to what they should be doing to get into position on the backswing. Their hands and club move in one direction, so consequently they are never in a position to make a coordinated inside-out downswing with the club, hands, arms and body fused together. Quite the reverse, in fact. At the finish of the backswing, in a poor position which permits them no balance or feel, they have to hit from the top. This they do by moving the right shoulder and arm to the outside, for, although this is a wrong source of power for golfers to use, it is the only one they can summon.

Developing a proper coil on the backswing with the hands, arms and body working together is not the easiest thing in the world for average golfers. The best short cut I have found is getting them to picture and feel that their heels remain in the same position from the time of address until long after the ball is contacted. If they can remember this, it is remarkable how quickly the entire pattern of their swing changes and they start building a good swing which delivers maximum speed at the bottom of the arc. and from the inside.

23

HERMAN PEERY

Cascades Golf Club, Hot Springs, Va.

Pulling Down and Through

Golfers who can play the game every day and who start off by having exceptional control of their body action—which the average golfer doesn't—can inaugurate the downswing with their hips. For the average player, though, the best way to launch the downswing is to pull down with your left arm. What sort of a pulldown is it? Well, as you have heard before, it is something like pulling the rope of a bell. Do you pull straight down? Not exactly. You should pull the butt of the club toward the ball.

Remember, this pulling down is done by the left arm. It's the controlling agent, and if you let it be you will escape the many troubles that result from trying to push the club down from the top with the right hand and the right shoulder. By pulling down with the left arm and keeping that arm straight you automatically bring the right arm into the proper hitting position: the elbow is leading and the upper arm comes in close to the body. The right hand then will be just where it should be when it uncocks into the ball.

Let me emphasize that, as far as conscious moves are concerned at the beginning of the downswing, limit this to the left arm and hand. They not only pull the club into position but they must keep pulling all the way through the swing until the left hand is hip-high on the follow-through. When you pull all the way through, you will finish high. It is the natural, inevitable result of the correct, strong swing.

61- **95533 Me**

49

24

HAROLD SARGENT

East Lake Country Club, Atlanta

Controlling the Right Hand

Many golfers, in learning to play, were taught to hit the ball with the left hand and let the right hand go along for the ride. In the last few years we have heard the conflicting instruction to hit the stuffings out of the ball with the right hand.

Actually, there is a danger in both. It is impossible to hit the ball with only the left hand, and in an attempt to do so the player will only impede his natural power. It is true also that the right hand—and, I would add, the right side of the body—can be correctly used only when the swing has been properly set up so that it can play its part in proper balance with the left.

Assuming the player has reached the top of the backswing correctly, the first movement is the turning of the left hip back toward the line of flight, and the weight is moved toward the left foot. This movement will pull the hands down to a waist-high position, with the club dropped on the inside. If this movement has been made correctly, the right elbow will be riding to the right hip, and the wrists will still be fully cocked. The right arm then begins to straighten and continues to straighten as the ball is struck. As the right arm is straightening, the wrist will release its tension, or "cock," and the right side of the body will turn toward the line of flight.

25

FRED HAWKINS

El Paso Country Club, Texas

The Flexed Left Leg

The legs should remain flexed at all times during the swing. On the backswing, the right leg shouldn't lock; it shouldn't even straighten. The same is true of the left leg on the forward part of the swing. There used to be a school of thought that claimed it was desirable to hit against a straight left leg. It is quite an incorrect principle.

If there has been any one thing that has bothered me most in my efforts to improve my swing and hit better shots, it has been getting away from a long-ingrained habit of straightening the left leg as I come into the ball. If your left leg straightens in the impact area, your left side pulls up. This stops the left side from turning as it should as you hit through the ball. It throws your swing off the proper line and it checks the speed of your swing. Even at the finish of your swing when the left leg is necessarily straight, it isn't locked.

The key for me in correcting this habit of straightening the left leg was thinking of "staying level." By this I mean the feeling I get that my legs and my knees remain level with each other, that there is no up-and-down motion by either until I have completed the swing. I concentrate on this and I just continue turning.

Incorrect: left leg locked

Correct: left leg flexed

26

BILL WOTHERSPOON

Southern Hills CC, Tulsa

The Late Hit

It is commonly known that strong, flexible hands and wrists often prove to be the difference between an average and a good player. Some specialized exercising can be done to tone up these golfing muscles and open the avenue to greater power. For example, hold the club in your left hand with the thumb on top of the shaft, the arm extended and parallel with the ground. Now, bending only the wrist, raise and lower the club. If you spend a few minutes daily doing this exercise you will be pleasantly surprised at how much your control over the club will improve in a very short time. This same exercise should be done with the right hand but not as frequently as with the left. The right is stronger to begin with, and we are attempting to balance the power.

With hands that are strong enough you can work toward the action from which length results. Maintaining a wrist break on the downswing until the hands are opposite the ball—the late hit —is the trademark of all good golfers. Getting into position for the late hit isn't too difficult. The skill comes in having the club face contact the ball squarely, and this is where many golfers fail. In this position just before impact, if the left hand were carried through the ball at the speed it was traveling at up to this point, the result would be a weak slice. It is here, however, just before impact, that the left hand begins to supinate, to turn over so that the palm will be facing up to the sky at the end of the swing. This action of the left hand causes the right to accelerate its speed enormously and carries the club head into the ball with maximum force.

Immediately after the ball is contacted—it is all part of one uninterrupted swing, of course—both arms continue on and through, with the right being the new leader, passing the left as the left begins to break at the elbow.

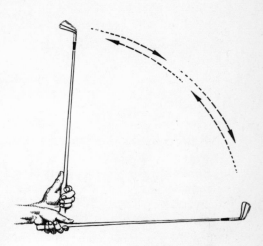

Exercise for developing
the hands and wrists

Position of hands
shortly after impact

27

GEORGE GORDON

Wannamoisett Country Club, Rumford, R. I.

Keeping the Left Arm Straight

Two of the most common errors that harry mediocre golfers is their failure to make a proper pivot and their tendency to let the left arm collapse before impact. Let us confine ourselves at this time to discussing the latter.

In a correct golf swing the left arm should be straight throughout an arc of some 180°: from shoulder height on the backswing through shoulder height on the swing-through. When the left arm collapses before impact, nine times out of 10 a pronounced slice results. Usually this collapse of the left arm is tied in with a premature turning of the right side and shoulder into the shot. When you rush the right side into the shot too soon, you throw your body and arms outside the correct line to the ball, and you are then compelled to swing from the outside in to contact the ball. That right side must stay relatively inactive until much later in the swing. Maintaining your left arm straight and firm through impact will delay the action of the right side until the proper time.

When I had the considerable pleasure of working with the Duke of Windsor on his game, one of the points we gave major attention to was this alliance of the straight left arm and the retarded right side. I think the duke's mastery of this was as important as any one feature in his improvement from a 100 golfer to a low-80s player.

56

Correct   **Incorrect**

57

28

BLANCHE SOHL

Ohio State University, Columbus, Ohio

Maximum Speed at Impact

Shortest definition of a golf swing: feel the weight of the club-head and swing it to produce maximum speed at the moment it hits the ball. If maximum speed has not been reached at impact, one is not hitting the ball.

Since the speed of the club head at the hit results finally from the wrists unbending and releasing, golfers should learn to delay this wrist action by pulling the hands into the ball on the forward swing with the wrists cocked until the last moment. This is the mark of a good swing.

Don't get ahead of yourself on the way down by throwing the club head away from the body, straightening out the wrists and the right arm. This is hitting too soon. Correctly, the hands should pull the club head to the ball. If you pull, the hands lead, and this keeps the wrists cocked and the right elbow folded up. It also preserves the greatest angle possible between the extended left arm and the club. On your pull, use all your strength, even your back muscles. The more pull, the more speed at impact and the more distance.

The transfer of the weight to the left foot and the unwinding of the body are tied in with the pull of the hands. Practice both at the same time. You can feel the resulting centrifugal force which hits or propels the ball. When you are playing, just swing and time this hit. You will be pulling to create maximum club head speed at the split second you make contact with the ball.

Incorrect   Correct

29

JIM TURNESA

PGA Champion, 1952

The Center of the Club Face

Anyone who has played golf seriously over a period of years (and has worked during that time to develop a sound swing and groove it) inevitably learns a tremendous lot about technique. This often can become a burden rather than a help. A golfer soon knows more about technique than he can ever hope to apply. His head can hold only so much. He cannot work on 10 things at one time without doing nine of them badly or, at any rate, less well than he might if he could concentrate all his attention on each of them —which he can't. I think the best way for any golfer to find his way out of the woods of overknowledge is to select one or two key parts of the swing which, if he executes them right, automatically insure that he will execute the other tied-in movements correctly.

Now, in this connection, the prime thing I concentrate on doing on the downswing is try to hit the ball in the center of the club face. There is nothing subtle or "inside" about this, I realize full well, and maybe that is its best recommendation. Simply working to hit the ball squarely with the middle of the face, I find, effects several important things. It smooths out the swing. It eliminates your doing a lot of things in the impact area you shouldn't do. It puts you into a position where you take your turf naturally with your irons. It bolsters your ability to stay down and over the ball as you come into it and strike it. I think of none of those things consciously. I think only of trying to hit the ball in the middle of the club face, and they are the results of this.

60

30

DENNY LAVENDER

Cedar Crest Golf Club, Dallas

The Hands Ahead of the Ball

One of the major points of difference in the swing of a fine golfer and the swing of a hacker is the position of the hands in relation to the club head at the instant of impact. The expert's hands are ahead of the ball. The hacker's are behind it.

This business of getting your hands ahead of the ball at impact is something like the explanation Jack Dempsey used to give for his tremendous hitting power. "I never hit a man on the chin," Dempsey used to say. "I hit through his chin right for the back of his head."

In golf, to get your hands through the ball, you must make a very conscious effort, just before impact, to get your hands a foot past the ball. You have to have the feeling that the club head is lagging well behind the hands as it approaches the ball. Actually, you can't get your hands a foot past the ball—they are never as far in front of the club head as you think—but by making a mental and physical effort to get them there, you will develop the correct action that allows you to hit through the ball with power. When your hands are behind the club head at impact, your power is lost and the best you can do is scoop the ball up weakly and improperly.

Correct—hands ahead   Incorrect—hands behind

31

JOE CANNON

Farmington CC, Charlottesville, Va.

Unwinding the Shoulders

Golfers frequently question me about what appears to be, in the swings of the best golfers, a sitting-down motion at the beginning of the downswing. I explain to them that they get this impression because a good golfer starts his hands down without unwinding his shoulders too soon. He wants to keep behind the ball with his shoulders as long as possible, arriving at the point of impact (*see large figure below*) with his shoulders parallel to the line of flight.

The small figure depicts a swing in which the shoulders have gotten out ahead of the ball before impact. This position is a very common one among average golfers. It is, as you can see, a weak position and one that is bound to result in a misdirected shot. Because the turn of the shoulders is a short turn compared to the wide sweep of the clubhead, it is easy to unwind the shoulders on the downswing before the clubhead completes its wider arc. I find that players who are experiencing this trouble can remedy it by keeping the right elbow close to the hip and the right shoulder well inside the line of flight.

Correct

Incorrect

65

32

PETER THOMSON

British Open Champion, 1954, 1955, 1956, and 1958

The Position of the Head

Although there is a good deal of variation in the methods and styles of the top tournament stars, there is one fundamental, I have observed, that is common to all of them. This is the head position at impact. At the moment they strike the ball, the head is positioned two or three inches behind the ball.

The large majority of average golfers, struggling to improve their games and more often than not finding this very difficult, have no idea where their head will be at impact. Many golfers habitually thrust their head ahead of the ball—and slice the shot. Others go to the opposite extreme. Their head is a good many inches behind the ball at impact—which encourages hooking. For that matter, it is not uncommon for golfers to alter the position of their head from day to day or even from swing to swing. This defeats the very thing they are trying to get: consistently accurate shot production based on a steadfast "groove."

The time to get the head set properly, of course, is at the start of the swing when you are addressing the ball. Line yourself up so that your head is two or three inches behind the ball and anchor it there surely, not tensely but firmly. It's a key position.

Head too far forward

Head too far back

Correct head position

ED FURGOL

U. S. Open Champion, 1954

The Right Elbow

When average golfers attend a major tournament, they are often struck by how long the top pros hit their shots and yet how easily they seem to swing at the ball. It takes effort to hit a golf ball—make no mistake about that—but a top pro's swing gives the impression of ease because his over-all timing is so precise. The power supplied by the body blends perfectly with the action of the hands.

In my case, the big thing in coordinating the body with the hands is keeping my right elbow tucked in close throughout the swing. By doing this, you tie in the action of the right side with the blow, and it's the right side that supplies the power behind a shot. To look at it the other way—if you have a floating right elbow, that gives your body no chance to get its contribution in. You're just slapping at the ball with your arms and your hands. The body is dormant. The leading pros naturally have different features they have worked on and continue to work on to achieve the integration of the body and the hands, but I pass the "tucked-in elbow" on to you because it is an essential part of every fine golfer's swing.

At the moment he makes contact with the ball, Ed
Furgol's right elbow is practically glued to his side

34

BABE ZAHARIAS

Guarding Against Slugging

During my career in golf I have seen countless poor shots caused by all kinds of errors. However, if I were asked to name the one chief error that undermines both the high- and low-handicap players, I would without hesitation nominate the almost universal striving for greater distance. Though I am a naturally long hitter, I have been subject myself to this fault from time to time, so I know from my own experience how disastrous it can be. By pressing for extra distance you hope to gain added yardage, but what happens is that you lose your balance and your timing, and all you gain are added woes: O.B. & P.L.—Out of Bounds and Probably Lost.

When I was a young girl just setting out in golf, I knew that my appeal for the spectators was my ability to smack the ball farther than a good many low-handicap men players. All I did for a while was to try to hit the ball a mile. I made my point. I was known as a long hitter. But I was so erratic that I wasn't really much of a golfer. It was only when I got some common sense and started to build a sound swing on a sound foundation that I began to become a player.

35

ED FURGOL
U. S. Open Champion, 1954

The Importance of Footwork

One very important part of the swing that is often overlooked by players who are striving to become better golfers is correct footwork. There is a temptation in golf, as in nearly every sport, to grow careless about your footwork when your hands are working well. Professionals soon learn, however, that if they allow their footwork to grow sloppy, their whole game will deteriorate. I know from my own experience, and from conversations with my fellow pros, that the days when it is easiest to play good golf shots are invariably those days when the feet are really doing their job.

What does their job consist of? Well, your footwork determines how well you pivot. In turn, the correctness of your pivot largely determines whether or not you will be in the right position to hit the ball to the best of your ability. There are two check points to establish clearly in regard to the role the feet play. First, at the top of your backswing, your left heel is raised off the ground and your weight transferred to your right side. Second, at the completion of your swing, the positions are reversed. The right heel is raised and the weight has been fully transferred to the left side.

Correct position, top of backswing

Correct position, completion of swing

Furgol's follow-through

36

AL BESSELINK

Grossinger, N. Y.

Keeping Square from Start to Finish

Everybody seems to have a different idea as to how the club face works going back and then forward. I used to think of shutting it on the backswing and working it from shut to open on the hitting stroke. More recently, I have discarded this idea and have been going with a different conception—and I have been hitting the ball much straighter than before and doing this much more easily.

The key to the approach I use now is to try to visualize, feel and maintain my club face so that it will be squarely parallel to my intended line of flight at three very important stages of the swing: halfway back, at the top, and halfway through the follow-through. For myself, it is easier to reach these positions with the club face squarely parallel if I think there is a wall behind me that is parallel to the line of flight. That wall is my point of reference. When I work with this thought in mind, I find that my hips and my club face close and later open at the same time. That's one of the reasons why Snead is so great and also so pretty to watch —everything is opening and closing together, in concert.

At address you want the back of your left hand to be squarely perpendicular to the line of flight. During the swing, you want that other type of squareness where the club face is squarely parallel to the line of flight at the points I mentioned. It puts you in wonderful positions throughout your whole swing and makes your impact solid and sweet.

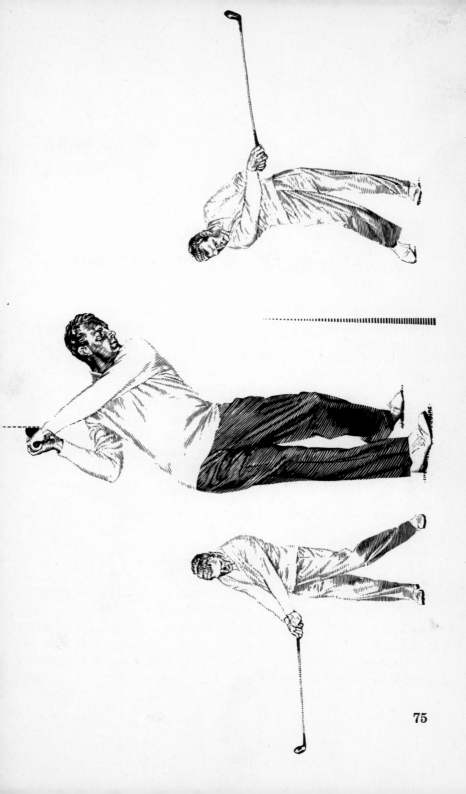

37

JULIUS BOROS

U. S. Open Champion, 1952

Staying Down Over the Shot

Early in every golfer's life-long tussle with the game he learns that there's a vast difference between 1) keeping your head down so that you have your eye on the ball at impact and 2) keeping your head down so that you finish your hitting action properly. "Staying down"—maintaining the proper head and body position during that split second after you have contacted the ball —is a tremendous factor in playing consistently accurate shots.

The simplest way to emphasize the importance of staying down is to remind you of what happens when you don't. When a golfer bobs his head up too quickly, he jerks up his hips and the upper part of his body along with his head. As a result, he generally pulls the shot to the left. This doesn't mean that you should exaggerate this anchoring of the head and body as you hit through the ball. If you do, you cannot move into the shot and finish it the way you should. Good golf, like all things, comes from striking the happy medium. Correcting one extreme by going to the other is no correction at all. Regular practice is the best (and only sure) way of gaining the feeling of when you are staying down long enough but not too long over your shots.

Julius Boros stays down over the ball as (above) he enters the hitting and (left) hits through the ball

38

GENE LITTLER

San Diego, Calif.

The Hit-Through

All golfers who want to improve their game are faced with a difficult problem: since it is impossible to work on all the phases of a swing, what are the key phases to concentrate on?

Speaking for myself, experience has taught me to remember (whatever else I may be thinking about in playing a shot) to be sure and hit through the ball—that is, to make sure that my club continues through the ball low along the ground on the line to the target. This is a very important part of the hitting action, this definite hit-through *for two feet or so* past the point where you make contact with the ball. You can take the club back wrong, or a little wrong, but if you hit through correctly on line, you will make out fairly well.

I stress this point because many average golfers of my acquaintance tend to think too much about parts of the golf swing that are much less essential. I believe that if they concentrated more on hitting through the ball, most average golfers would find themselves playing better golf shots consistently.

The wide arc of Gene Littler's swing as he hits through the ball

39

MARY LENA FAULK

Glen Arven CC, Thomasville, Ga.

Strengthening the Left Arm

Recently, when I was reading Henry Cotton's *This Game of Golf,* a book that delighted me with its many provocative thoughts on that inexhaustible subject, I was particularly struck by a short chapter about practicing with the left hand only.

Being a great believer in timing and rhythm, which a strong left side produces, I have taken Mr. Cotton's advice and have started practicing a left-hand swing with the wedge. It tells you a great deal. You can feel with marvelous clarity everything that happens in the swing, and you get a good feeling of contact with the ball. Right from the start, you discover another important plus: practice with the left hand alone makes you finish your swing. You can't possibly hit the ball unless you do.

Swinging with the left arm teaches an equally significant lesson. You find out the role the controlling left side plays in every phase of the swing and exactly how the movements of the left arm relate to the other parts of the body. To start with, it compels you to get set up correctly at address with your feet and legs positioned strongly. Otherwise, you can't even begin a golf swing. Throughout the swing, it reinforces facts you had previously known but never appreciated so keenly. You are more certain than ever, for instance, that when you sway off the ball you can't get back to it. In the end, when you begin to swing with both hands again, you find that everything—everything that should be in the swing—has become more clearly defined.

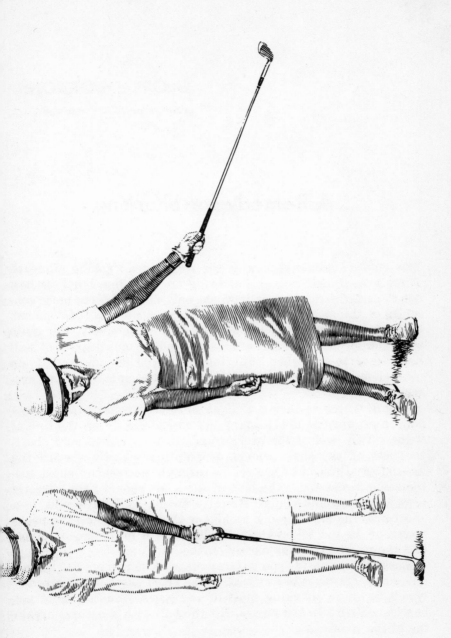

40

GEORGE GORDON
Wannamoisett CC, Rumford, R. I.

A Remedy for Shanking

The shank, I would reckon, is the worst of all golfing ailments. There are explicit causes that bring on shanking, but it is best not to describe them since it would only make players more conscious of things they are better off to have no mind of. One can be explicit, however, about the remedy for the shank. For quite a few decades now, golfers of all sorts and various degrees of skill have come to me when suffering with this malady and, I am pleased to say, have benefited almost on the spot from my prescription.

The first step in curing a shank is for the golfer to swing the club in an upright arc, keeping his hands exactly on the line of flight. At the end of the backswing, which should be very short, the butt of the shaft should be pointing directly toward the ground. At the end of the follow-through, necessarily short too, the same is also true: the butt of the shaft should point directly toward the ground. This corrective swing, as I have said, is a short one, the hands going no higher than the hips on the backswing or on the follow-through. There is a minimum of pivot, and the weight remains mostly on the left foot.

These steps provide you with a firm track to run on, but there's one point that must be stressed. On all short shots to the green—which is where shanking most often occurs—the ball must not be scooped with locked wrists. Hit the ball with a natural breaking of the wrists.

41

PHIL TAYLOR

Victoria Golf Club, Victoria, B. C.

Stepping on the Spot

People say it different ways: "Keep your head down." "You picked your head up." "Keep your eye on the ball." "Just hit the ball, we'll watch it." The phrases are familiar and have been with us since the beginning of golf. Undoubtedly, they will continue to be trotted out as long as the game is played. For looking up to see where the ball is going, even before it is hit, is the most common fault in golf.

The best cure for the bad habit is to develop a superior swing. If you are on balance and in position, it is natural to look at the ball. However, for the average player who has his limitations, I recommend a practice I call "stepping on the spot." At address, and while he is launching his swing, the golfer should focus on the ball. As he hits through it, he should keep his eye on the spot where the ball was. Then, while he is still over the ball at the completion of his swing, his next move should be to step on the spot where the ball was, with his right foot, before lifting his head to see where the ball went. The move may seem awkward, but it will pay off.

You can't do anything else but keep your head down if you are concentrating on stepping on the spot. You can view this as a cure for shanking too. During the 50 years I have been teaching the game, I have found stepping on the spot an excellent remedy for both faults.

84

85

42

ED DUDLEY

Augusta National Golf Club, Ga.

Maintaining Rhythm and Tempo

The average golfer, when trying for extra distance, attempts to speed up his swing and hit the ball harder and faster with his hands and body. Most of the time when he does this, he hits too soon with his hands and body, and thus destroys the rhythm and tempo of his swing. As a result, he loses both distance and accuracy. Rhythm and tempo must be maintained at all times, even when you're playing the most difficult shot. This is why our star players spend countless hours working on them.

What, then, do these star players do to obtain extra distance? Instead of trying to swing faster and hit the ball harder, they just turn their left shoulder a little bit more to the right on the backswing than they normally do. It's very much like the pitcher in baseball who reaches back a little farther than usual when he wants to get a little added zip on his fast ball. It gives your muscles that little extra stretch that produces that little extra power without destroying the vital rhythm and even tempo which are so essential to all good golf swings.

Ed Dudley urges golfers to develop rhythm and tempo
by practicing them regularly

43

BILL SHIELDS

Thorny Lea Golf Club, Brockton, Mass.

Warming Up

Whenever you can, hit out a few balls before you begin your round. And use your head when you warm up. There's nothing gained by taking out your driver and just seeing how much beef you can put into a swing. What you want to do is to get a good sound swing started, to get your shots moving out there with a pattern that has some character to it.

Start your warmup with the mashie, the five-iron. I'll tell you why. It encourages a controlled swing in which you pivot properly and use your hands the way you should. If you start with a niblick, you're too apt to develop a pattern that doesn't tie body action and arm action together. You don't swing. And if you rush right off with a wooden club or a long iron, instinctively you try to hit the ball for distance before your swing is ready for it. Now with the five-iron you're just trying to get the ball out there 150 yards or so, so there's no tendency to press or to rush it. Then, once you've established a good pattern and rhythm for your swing, you can change to a long iron or hit a few woods and strengthen this groove.

Fifty-odd years ago we used to practice at Oakley by hitting five-irons to a pail down the practice fairway. I still think it is the best stick in the bag either for beginning a quick preround warmup or a more intensive session on the practice fairway.

44

FRED NOVAK

St. Andrews Golf Club, Hastings-on-Hudson, N. Y.

Starting with the Left Foot

When you are at a course with weekend golfers, you are struck by the high percentage of players who swing at the ball and in the same motion let their whole weight shift back. They want to hit through, we know that, but they simply can't. Because of what has gone before in their swing, they have lost the means to follow through.

Too many golfers make the mistake of taking the club back with their hands only. They want to hit the ball really hard. You can see it in their shoulders. But that is exactly where they defeat their purpose. As the hands whip the club back, the left knee sags out and the player stiffens his left leg. On the downswing, consequently, the left leg tips him back toward the right just as he begins to straighten the leg. He is forced finally to swivel his body feebly around and lash at the ball as he falls back. He's trapped.

The correct execution of a golf swing depends on the timing of the hands and feet. They should go back as one piece. The golfer will put himself on the right track if he realizes that the left foot actually starts the swing. Specifically, it is a steady push from the outside toward the inside of the left leg. The push starts the hands and arms moving back, and with the correct synchronization. When you swing down to hit the ball you will be on balance and completely relaxed. If you begin with your feet and hands together, they will stay together in your swing.

Incorrect

45

PETER THOMSON
British Open Champion, 1954, 1955, 1956, and 1958

The Take-Away

An extremely critical part of the golf swing—I cannot overstate its importance—is the take-away, the action at the very start of the swing in which the hands take the club back and the swing begins to take its form.

Let me state as positively and as plainly as possible what a golfer should strive for in the take-away. First, the club should be taken back neither by the left hand nor the right hand but by *both* hands, working together. The club should be taken back neither outside nor inside but straight back, right on the line of flight. The arms should be just a little short of extended, sort of semirelaxed, as opposed to being overextended or pushed out.

If you start the swing with a correct take-away, the battle is half done. You will automatically fall into a correct position at the top of the backswing, and knowing this helps you eliminate the thinking you would otherwise do about attaining that correct position at the top. In a few words, then, a correct take-away is the key, as I see it, to simplifying the complicated business of building a sound golf swing.

Wrong, inside the line

Wrong, outside the line

Correct

93

46

BYRON NELSON

U. S. Open Champion, 1939

Going Back

The average golfer is subject to three fundamental faults when he takes the club back: (*1*) picking the club up too quickly with his hands, rather than swinging the club back along the line; (*2*) pulling the club up too close to the body; and (*3*) starting the body action before the hands and the golf club start to move—which pulls the body out of line and forces the golfer into an unbalanced chopping action.

When I first began playing, I brought the club back too close on the backswing, and this caused me to hook and shank. To overcome this fault, I drew a mental line straight back from the ball, and also in front of the ball, to reinforce my awareness of the line of flight—the line I intended the ball to travel. Then I worked on drawing the club back along that line.

Today my habit is to pick an object in the foreground that is situated on the line of flight—a tree or a bunker or a house. Then I take the club back straight from that object and the ball. To check my backswing in practice, I stick a tee about six or eight inches behind the ball on the intended line of flight. And when I draw the club back I can check to see whether the club hits the tee squarely or whether it tips or shanks it.

Incorrect: club pulled up
too close to the body

Correct: club is taken back on straight
line from the ball, with the hands, the
club, and the body moving cohesively

47

MARILYNN SMITH

French Lick, Ind.

The Role of the Right Elbow

My dad used to say that there were three times when the right elbow should be down: eating, riding a horse and swinging the golf club back.

At the start of the backswing, the straight left arm and the turning left shoulder must begin their critical functions correctly, but just as important for me in getting my swing on the right track is flexing my right elbow away from the ball. This flexing of the elbow gives me the feeling of wanting to turn—it really sets up my turn. It works in fusion with my shoulders and hips. Formerly, when I used to give my primary attention at the start of the backswing to bringing both hands back emphatically on the line, my arms and body worked independently of each other. I never felt as joined together as I wanted to.

Throughout the backswing, the flexed right elbow points to the ground. When you practice this movement and get it down right, you don't have to think of cocking your wrists going back. You think of cocking your elbow. I only want to add one word of caution. When golfers work on any new move, they are apt to forget that they must still pay attention to the real permanent fundamentals of every golf swing; in other words, when you work on flexing your right elbow away from the ball, don't forget that the left arm and shoulder must still share in the control of the swing.

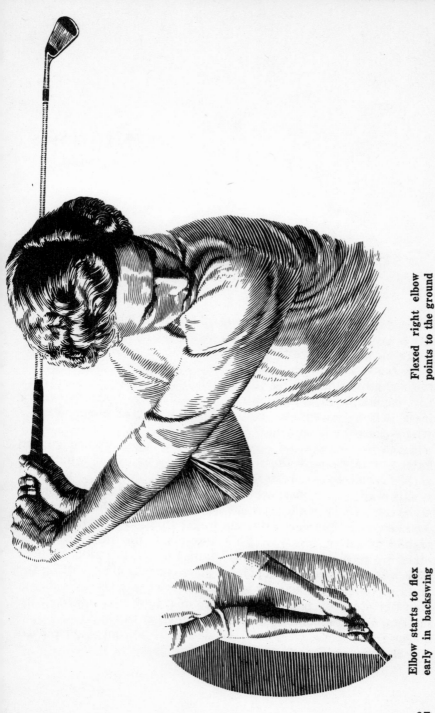

Flexed right elbow
points to the ground

Elbow starts to flex
early in backswing

48

PATTY BERG

St. Andrews, Ill.

Getting the Right Hip Out of the Way

Since women don't have as powerful hands as men do, they can't get away with a poorly executed swing nearly so well. In order to develop adequate hitting power, a woman must master really good footwork and body action; and she must tie these together with rhythm and timing. The catch here is that comparatively few women seem to understand the difference between correct body action—based on pivoting—and incorrect body action— where the sway is ruinous.

Since the word pivot seems to confuse most women golfers rather than present them with a clear picture of what they should do, perhaps a better way to get the point across is to put it this way: on the backswing, you do not slide your body laterally from left to right, *you coil your body away from the ball.* The key to coiling correctly, the way I think of it, is to get the right hip out of the way. This movement, the rotation of the right hip to the rear, is actually started by the left side. If there ever was a shortcut to proper body action, this is it: getting the right hip out of the way. If you do that, you won't sway and you won't be stuck off balance at the top of a faulty backswing with nothing but a feeble pair of hands to chop at the ball.

One thing more. Keep your head still. If you move your head off the ball, you'll probably move your body along with it.

Incorrect:
the lateral sway

Correct:
the right hip rotates

The strong coiled position
at the top of the backswing

99

49

FRANK STRANAHAN

Crystal River, Fla.

The End of the Backswing

On all shots from the chips through the irons to the woods, always try to have a little wrist action at the end of the backswing. Let me make clear that the wrist action I speak of has nothing to do with the downswing; it's entirely concerned with the finish of the backswing. This small suffix of wrist action introduces a little lightness to your swing at a very important point. Its value cannot be overemphasized because the end result is that it gives you that minute thing called timing.

Let me explain this a bit further. If the golf club is swung so that it has the free release of centrifugal force, the ball can be hit truer and with greater club head speed than if the golfer tries to hold the club on line, to steer the ball, as he hits through it. If a golfer's grip comes up dead at the top of the backswing, however, he can't make a correct dynamic swing: he has to leap and jump to hit. This is the reason why that touch of wrist action at the top of the backswing is so valuable. It reaffirms the life of your swing and your timing. While you're taking this wrist action, your body goes forward and out of the way (as you can observe in the swings of most of the top professionals) and the golfer is able to perform the most nearly perfect arc on the downswing. In short, this little bit of wrist action is the key to developing a great deal of club head speed without effort.

50

RUTH JESSEN
Inglewood CC, Kenmore, Wash.

Holding Your Head Steady

The improvement in my game in recent months I attribute to a good degree to finally learning to hold my head steady.

For four years I had trouble doing that. If you are right-eyed—as I am—and cock your head to the right as you go back, there's no way you can see the ball. If you're left-eyed, as Sam Snead and Louise Suggs are, for example, cocking your head is fine for you. Right-eyed golfers, however, must learn to hold the head in a fixed position over the ball.

When players are working on refining their backswing, they sometimes unconsciously pick up the habit of turning their heads to the right to check certain positions of the hands and the club-head. Be certain you avoid this not uncommon pitfall. For another thing, don't become overimpressed when you hear that the top players can hit the ball without looking at it. They can, but when they go off their games it is probably because they have taken their heads and eyes off the ball.

Is there any simple prescription that will enable you to hold your head still? I think there is. Practice closing your bad eye. It will steady not only your head but your entire swing as well.

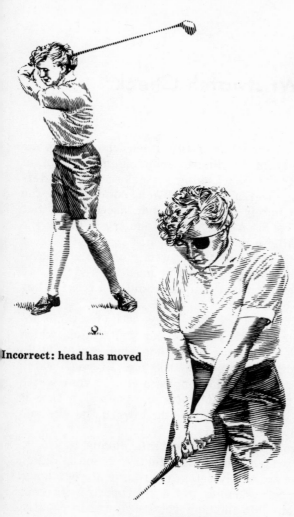

Incorrect: head has moved

Correct: head still

Train your good eye

103

51

PAT DEVANY

Grosse Ile Golf & Country Club, Mich.

The Wristwatch Check

For some reason or other, nine out of 10 women who come to me for instruction suffer from an almost epidemic misconception about the golf swing. On the backswing they close the face terribly. They take a big, overfull swing. Then, coming into the ball, they ease up and barely hit it. The men are at the other extreme. They take too short a backswing, then try to knock the cover off the ball. With both men and women, I try to get across that it is impossible to perform the correct, integrated movements on the downswing unless the golfer goes back right, and I spend a lot of time getting them to understand and feel the key motions of taking the club back.

Here there is one simple check that everyone understands instantly and profits from. In this you use your wristwatch, which is conveniently on the left wrist, as your guide. On a correct backswing, when your hands are hip-high, the face of your watch should face your instructor standing opposite you. If your watch is facing the ground at that point you know your club face is closed. Conversely, if your watch is facing toward the sky you know your club face is wide open.

When you go out and practice, concentrate during the backswing on having your watch face an imaginary person standing opposite you. Try to be agreeably relaxed throughout your body, for it encourages your left shoulder to tie in properly with your arm's movement. If your left shoulder rotates upward properly, your right shoulder will stay down and you will have to strike the ball a descending blow—which is what you want to do.

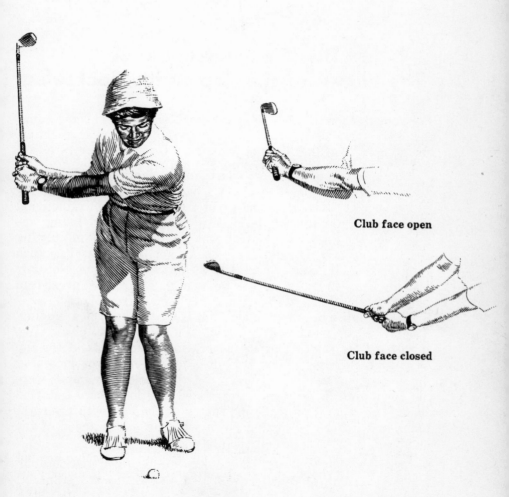

Club face open

Club face closed

52

TOMMY ARMOUR
U. S. Open Champion, 1927

The Hands at the Top of the Backswing

While playing at Winged Foot Golf Club recently my friend Claude Harmon, the pro there, gave me an invaluable tip.

Claude is one of the most observant students of the game, as well as one of the finest teachers. I had not been living up to my newspaper reputation as the great iron player, and although I knew I was standing at the ball correctly, that my timing was good, and the groove of the club was good, I was still not hitting the ball properly. I could not seem to get the necessary punch into the shot. Hole after hole, I was short of the green. Not only was my game hurt, but so was my vanity. The alleged great iron player was not able to hit even a single good iron shot.

Then at lunch one day Claude said, "I know what you are doing, Tommy. Shall I tell you?" I said, "Please, Claude, please give it to me." He said, "You are separating your hands at the top of your backswing." Now that does not mean I was loosening my fingers, but as you will see by the illustration, my hands were not remaining in the same interrelated position where I started them. The separation made me snatch at the ball with my right hand, and instead of coming down with my hands ahead of the clubhead, they were actually behind it.

This is an extremely common fault. If your iron shots are not going out with their usual zip, I recommend that you check your hands at the top. It immediately cured my troubles, and I know it will help you.

Top of backswing

Incorrect

Correct

107

53

SHELLEY MAYFIELD

Meadow Brook Club, Westbury, N. Y.

The Left Heel

Among our fine professionals, it has become standard practice—as uniform as the grip—to raise the left heel only a shade on the backswing. When they are playing the six-iron through the wedge, the left heel never leaves the ground. On a full shot with a driver, calling for the fullest pivot, the greatest exchange of weight, and the longest arc, the left heel is never lifted more than an inch and a half off the ground. There are, in fact, a few players, myself among them, who prefer to play all their shots without ever raising the left heel off the ground.

My reason for calling this to your attention is that most average golfers have the habit of lifting the left heel far too much on the backswing, sometimes as high as five inches. This tends to pull the golfer's head "off the ball" as he nears the top of the backswing. Furthermore, when you lift the left heel too high, nine out of ten times on the downswing you will return it to the right or left of the position it occupied when you started your swing. Replacing your heel an inch to the right or left can change your line of flight as much as twenty yards. On the other hand, raising the left heel the bare minimum is a major step toward achieving consistency and greater firmness at impact.

Incorrect: heel lifted much too high

Correct: heel lifted only slightly

54

BETSY RAWLS

Country Club of Spartansburg, S. C.

The Shoulder Turn

An exceedingly high percentage of the women who play golf are slicers. They slice chiefly because they bring the club back with an improper shoulder turn. As they near the top of the backswing, instead of continuing to swing the club back and to turn the shoulders easily, they have a tendency to push their shoulders and arms up. Then, before they have completed the backswing, they start the downswing. Not only is their timing thrown off, but starting the club down from a position at the top where it points to the left side of the fairway is the invariable prelude to coming into the ball from the outside and cutting across it— slicing.

At the top of the backswing, the club, ideally, should be directly parallel to your intended line of flight, pointing, as it were, right at the target. If you have made a sufficient turn, your shoulders will be square. One excess, of course, is as bad as the other, and I would caution you about overturning the shoulders. This places the club in a position at the top where it is pointing to the right side of the fairway. A hooked shot generally results, for, if you overturn going back, you have to overturn to get back to the ball.

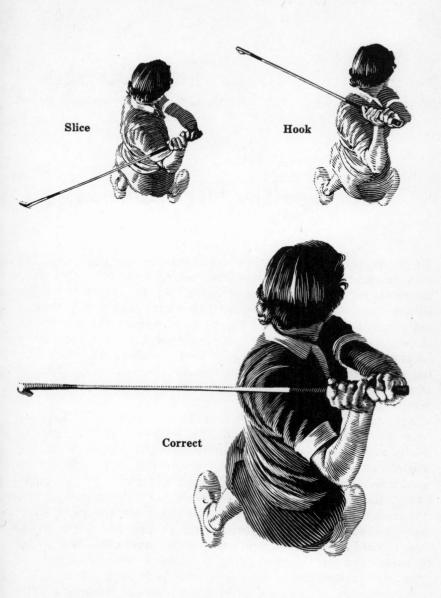

Slice

Hook

Correct

111

55

SHELLEY MAYFIELD

Meadow Brook Club, Westbury, N. Y.

The Right Shoulder and Elbow

Many average golfers I have watched defeat their purpose at the very beginning of the stroke: they address the ball with their shoulders level, the right raised as high as the left. If you think things over for a moment, you will realize that the left hand grips the club a full hand's length higher along the shaft than the right hand does. With both shoulders level and both arms extended, it follows that, if your left arm is extended comfortably, the right will be strained and rigid. This is exactly opposite to what you want in golf: you want a straight left arm and a relaxed right arm.

At address a golfer's right shoulder should hang three or four inches lower than his left. This enables the right arm to be in a relatively relaxed position. In turn, the right elbow, when it is not overextended stiffly at address, will be in a position where it can perform its correct function. On the backswing, the right elbow "folds" close to the body so that, at the top of the backswing, the straight line between the right wrist and elbow points vertically toward the ground and not horizontally toward the horizon. It is really quite impossible for a golfer to move into the proper hitting position if his right elbow is "floating" incorrectly at the top of the backswing.

The position of address is an active part of the swing. The arms, hands, and shoulders naturally seek to return to the approximate position of address when they enter the hitting area.

Incorrect

Correct

56

AL MENGERT

Echo Lake Country Club, Westfield, N. J.

Hand Position on the Backswing

A great many players make golf (which is a hard enough game to begin with) much harder for themselves when they break their wrists on the way back. About halfway through the backswing they lay their wrists off on a lateral plane, pushing the hands well behind the body in this same motion. This puts the golfer in an awkward and weak position. His club head, incidentally, is wide open. He has a terrible time on the downswing. He has to roll the wrists over and make many other adjustments in a small space of time in order to come into the ball. On the other hand, when your hands are properly positioned on the backswing you don't have to adjust them on the downswing, and this makes coming into the ball incomparably easier.

The average player, I think, falls into this incorrect hand and wrist movement on his backswing when he tries to flatten his swing with a deliberate action of the hands instead of flattening his swing with his shoulder turn. If most average golfers could study photographs of their swing, they would be amazed to see how often they make no appreciable shoulder turn going back. A proper shoulder turn, of course, affects many important aspects of the swing. Among other things, it takes good care of the hands: when you rotate your shoulders the full way, your hands just have to come up into the correct position.

Correct

Incorrect

115

Part III

Hitting the Ball from Tee to Green

57

GEORGE BAYER

Gleneagles CC, Lemont, Ill.

Relaxing on the Drive

Only seasoned golfers appreciate the fact that the way to hit the ball longer is not to hit it harder but to hit it better. The average golfer doesn't quite believe this. He is all for turning on sheer muscular force. Watch him on the tee, and you will see him time after time making the same moves as he sets himself to blast an extra-long one: he widens his stance; he drops his right shoulder into what feels like a more power-producing position; as that shoulder moves lower the right arm and hand move down low with it. With these "adjustments" he has started to move off the ball and out of the correct balanced position at which all good swings are inaugurated.

No professional is merely indulging in persiflage when he states that most average golfers fail to get the distance they're capable of because they fail to take advantage of their natural abilities— timing and coordination. To do so, you must be genuinely relaxed as you start the stroke and let the various components swing into the swing smoothly and evenly. If you hurry the backswing you scramble your coordination. So start relaxed and stay relaxed. Keeping your head steady will help you in this. The swing revolves around the head. Then, as you go back, you can turn the hips and knees nice and easy and progress naturally from that point. Work for an integrated swing. Distance results from one and so does accuracy, without which distance is all too often a Pyrrhic victory.

Correct

Incorrect

119

58

LIONEL HEBERT

PGA Champion, 1957

The Pivot in Driving

I've known people who've played golf quite seriously for 25 years and who have never given their driving the time and attention it needs. Driving is as important as any part of the game. You do it on 14 of the 18 holes. Most of your great players were (and are) skillful drivers who set themselves up on tee after tee so that they maintained a steady tee-shot production. It was the key to their scoring, for consistent driving puts a player continuously in a position to put his iron approach up close.

Golf has so much tension involved in it that a wise player wants to eliminate as much thinking as possible and learn to rely, if he can, on one single master motion. In driving, as I have experienced it, the key is working sedulously on a proper pivot until it is almost second nature. A good pivot does three things for you: it gives you good balance; it produces more power with less effort; and it automatically increases your accuracy, which results from a combination of balance and power. I cannot over-emphasize how strongly I advise every person who wants to drive better to give priority to the development of a really fine pivot, one that is a natural turn of the body, with everything—legs, hips, shoulders—moving in proper synchronization. From a good pivot you develop into a good player. This is where you begin.

59

ALEX TIBBLES

Lima Golf Club, Lima, Peru

Staying Behind the Ball

The most difficult thing for the average golfer to do, in my opinion, is to stay behind the ball. He has a tendency to move ahead of the ball with the body, and in doing so he develops an outside-in swing which causes such familiar troubles as slicing, shanking, and topping. This is particularly true on the drive, which so many players try to hit with too much power.

Learning to stay behind the ball can be facilitated by a practice exercise in which the player tees the ball somewhat higher than usual. If you can't get hold of extra-long tees, then simply dig the regular tee into the ground the minimum amount necessary to secure it. When the ball is teed up this high, the player must literally swing from the inside out in order to hit it at all solidly. In addressing a ball which is teed higher than usual, the player should set the club head about three inches behind the ball, for this will help him to hit through it squarely.

The value of this practice exercise, as you will soon discover, is that it emphasizes the right hitting habits. It forestalls moving the head and upper part of the trunk out of position and ahead of the ball before impact. It militates against a forward sway with the legs and thighs. You will find that, with your body properly behind the ball, you will have less of a tendency to steer the ball and will finish your swing much higher. I think you will also discover that, when you go out on the course after this training exercise, you will repeat this correct hitting action when the ball is teed its normal height.

Incorrect

Correct

60

CHICK HARBERT

PGA Champion, 1954

Driving for Distance

Let's be honest about it—one of the chief thrills of golf is smashing a long tee shot far, far down the fairway. In no other ball-and-stick or ball-and-racquet game can the average player propel the ball the distance he can in golf. No wonder the inward delight and satisfaction is intense when you hit one of your best drives.

Other factors being consistent, the length of the arc of your swing governs your distance off the tee. The fuller you pivot, the longer the arc. The longer the arc, the greater the club head speed you generate. The greater the speed as it strikes, the farther the ball will travel—I repeat, other factors being consistent.

There are certain cautions and suggestions I feel I should advance for golfers interested in increasing their distance. 1) Don't try to lengthen the arc of your swing unless your muscular flexibility, age, weight and sight give you the athletic ability to do so. 2) Your grip must be firm but not rigid. 3) The head remains securely anchored at all times during the swing. 4) The development of a fuller pivot cannot be achieved if you allow your body to sway. In fact, swaying makes efficient pivoting impossible.

124

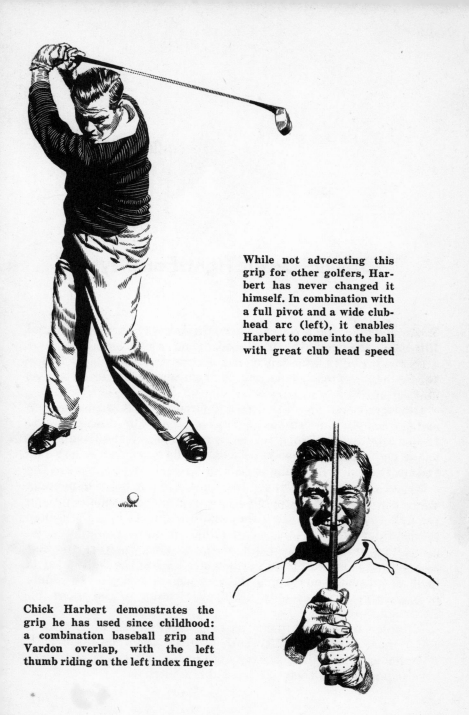

While not advocating this grip for other golfers, Harbert has never changed it himself. In combination with a full pivot and a wide clubhead arc (left), it enables Harbert to come into the ball with great club head speed

Chick Harbert demonstrates the grip he has used since childhood: a combination baseball grip and Vardon overlap, with the left thumb riding on the left index finger

61

LIONEL HEBERT

PGA Champion, 1957

Driving Down Tight Fairways

When he is playing a course where the fairways are narrow and tree-lined, the man who is a good driver really shines. A good driver is a player who can plan a certain type of shot to fit the requirements of each hole and then go ahead and execute that plan.

He doesn't step up on the tee and simply aim down the middle and try to split the fairway. What he does is aim down one side of the fairway and work the ball in. If most of the trouble lies to the right of the fairway, he will aim down the safer left side and hit the ball with a slight fade that brings it back toward the center of the fairway. Conversely, when the left is the dangerous side, he will aim down the right, away from the trouble, hitting the ball with a slight draw that again brings it into the center of the fairway. When he takes either of these two routes, he gives himself the whole width of the fairway to work the ball into. Say the fairway is 40 yards wide. He has the full 40 yards to shoot at, twice the room of the man who aims down the middle and so leaves himself only a 20-yard leeway to the rough on either side.

In order to execute these tee-shot tactics, it stands that a golfer must have the ability both to draw and fade his drives. This amounts to skill of a very high order, but the best drivers have it, and it sets them off from the other boys.

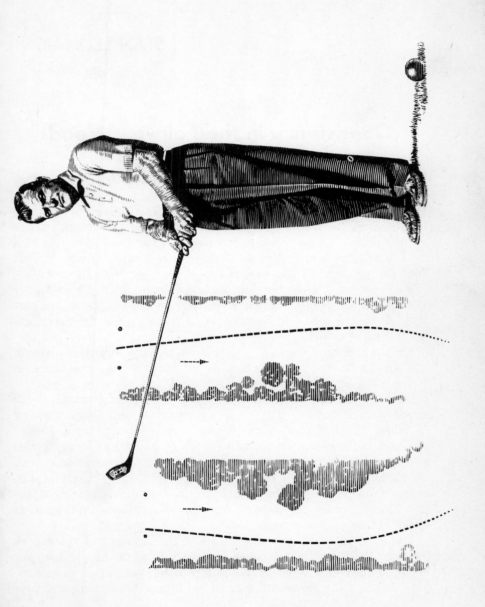

62

STAN LEONARD

Vancouver, B. C.

Consistency in the Fairway Woods

When you're playing your fairway woods keep well in mind that as long as you overswing you cannot have control over where the ball is going. Part and parcel of overswinging, brought on by the hunt for distance, is an overshifting of the weight to the right foot on the backswing and then forward onto the left foot on the downswing. It breeds chronic inaccuracy. When the left foot jumps way off the ground, as it will when you overswing, it's almost an impossible job for a golfer to hold himself over the ball as he should. And the extra power you think you are getting from the extra movement is in reality only an extra expenditure of effort.

On the fairway woods you should, to use the expression we do in Canada, "trap" the left foot. What this means, in essence, is to limit its activity as far as possible. Don't allow it to work. I believe a man can hit a ball at least as far (and certainly with much more accuracy) if he develops a precise, less lengthy swing in which the left foot is not freely released going back. In the old days both the American and English players had looser styles and the players had to work very hard when they went in search of distance. Today we realize much more clearly that distance comes from getting a full shoulder pivot and from delayed action timing which depends on the player's balance and position as he comes into the ball.

My idea on wood shots is to allow the hands full release at impact. You can't work over the ball if your hands are too locked. And you will not arrive in a position very often to release your hands fully if you indulge in too long a backswing and lose your position over the ball.

"Trap" the left foot

63

GENE SARAZEN

U. S. Open Champion, 1922 and 1932

Shallow-Faced Fairway Woods

For a good many golfers today, there is apparently only one sea-son: winter. Even when the calendar states it is July, they play winter rules, helping themselves to preferred lies before each shot from the fairway. In the long run they are not helping themselves at all. To develop sound hand action, the secret of good golf, a player must learn to hit his shots from all varieties of lies. Besides, that is the game.

When it comes to the woods especially, the average golfer takes a preferred lie almost automatically because he has no confidence the club will get the ball up into the air. Here I would strongly recommend that he use fairway woods with shallow faces. For one thing, the club head can get down into the ball on a snug lie far better than a deep-faced club head can. For another, on a normal lie, the shallow face rides below the top of the ball, and this gives you the wonderful feeling that you can't miss getting that ball up. Call it optics if you want, but it will help you to move into the complete swing with greater confidence and style.

I am always a little surprised today when I find myself re-ferred to as an outstanding fairway wood player, for I certainly wasn't when I started my career. I do know, though, that after I changed from deep-faced to shallow-faced woods, I became far more consistent and accurate.

Shallow face

Deep face

Ball rides visibly over
the top of face of shal-
low-faced three wood

131

64

WIFFI SMITH

St. Clair, Mich.

Balance and the Four-Wood

On the women's professional circuit, with tournaments scattered throughout the country, a player spends a good portion of her time driving on the road. Those hours behind the wheel can make you tense, and when you arrive at the site of the next tournament, it takes some loosening up. On the practice tee what I do first is to get two or three clubs and swing them together easily, as a batter does in baseball. Then I get my four-wood. There's more feeling in the four-wood for me than in any other club. I like the feel of the club head—it has the weight on the bottom. Along with this, I think it has the best over-all balance of any club. I find it the easiest to swing and the easiest to hit with. I can sting the ball with the four-wood.

When I'm shaking the kinks out swinging the four-wood, I have a very definite idea of the swing I want and the feel of the swing I want: I want to get everything moving smoothly. Accordingly, balance is what I work for. At the forefront of my concentration is the importance of finishing every shot on balance, not to fall back, for if you have the right balance everything comes through faster. In this connection, I find a tip given to me early in my career by my old club pro, Tom Garcia, to be very valuable, and I pass it on to you with the hope that you will really try it. When you are hitting out practice balls, hold your finish after each shot until the ball hits the ground. Simply having this thought in mind seems to encourage a swing that is integrated and balanced from start to finish.

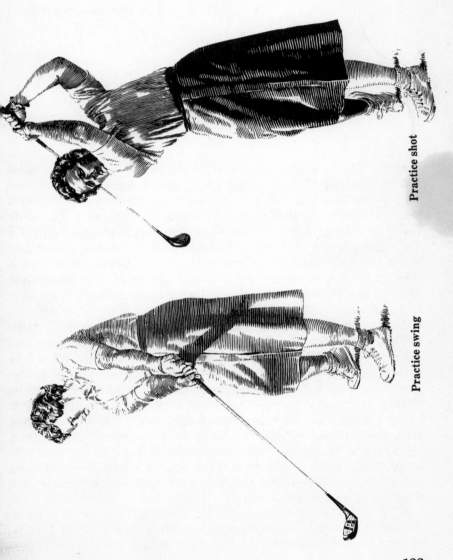

Practice shot

Practice swing

133

65

BYRON NELSON

U. S. Open Champion, 1939

The Long Irons

Because the face of a long iron—the number one, two, or three —has so very little loft, it leads players to fear that they will not get the ball up into the air. The usual result is that the player tends to lift up with his body in the act of hitting the ball, instead of making sure that he stays down with the ball. And far from helping you to get the ball nicely into the air, this lifting up of the body produces a low-flying shot and very often a slice. The good players all make a conscious effort to stay down over the ball and to reserve the use of the hands until the club is really in the hitting area.

In my observation, the other chief error most golfers make with a long iron is one that apparently stems from that frequently repeated instruction to take a shorter swing with a long iron than with a wood. Many players consequently take less than a full pivot on the backswing, and then make matters worse by trying to throw in some extra body action at contact. The first thing a player should remember is that the swing with the long iron is no different from the swing with the wood, except that, the shaft being shorter, the golfer must stand closer to the ball. Come back with a full backswing and a complete pivot, and when you move into the ball you will have all the power you need—and you will know it.

Correct: full back-
swing and pivot

Incorrect: restricted
backswing and pivot

66

WIFFI SMITH

St. Clair, Mich.

Trusting the Long Irons

Most women players are apt to overuse their woods. They favor them because woods swing more easily than irons. Also the faces of fairway woods, as opposed to the long irons, have more loft on them and give women confidence that they will get the ball into the air. When the average woman player does occasionally use her two-iron, three-iron or four-iron, she feels she is struggling with clubs that might very well dribble the ball along the ground. To compensate, she tries to scoop the ball up—and that is fatal.

To play good golf, you have to develop good hand action. You can do this best by playing the irons, which are shorter than the woods and require greater control. In learning to play the irons the first step is to gain confidence in the club head. It will get the ball up for you if you give it a chance and if you don't interrupt your swing as you come into the ball. Give up the idea of trying to scoop the ball. It will rise nicely if you drive the club head into and through the ball.

For myself, I like to feel that I am going to drive the ball right into the ground. Actually, you are hitting through the ball, but thinking in terms of hitting down on it creates the correct arc for your swing and moves your hands into a position where they are capable of live action, the kind of action that makes for a beautiful shot, which is what you want.

On the long irons, the left hand should grip the
club a bit more firmly than on the other shots

67

ART SMITH
The Camargo Club, Cincinnati

Checking Your Long-Iron Play

Many otherwise competent golfers have great difficulty in playing their long irons. In a large way this comes from a lack of confidence in their ability to handle these shots. Since no one can teach confidence, the best assistance one can give, I think, is to explain to these golfers how they can examine their swing for the errors which most commonly throw off long-iron play and, consequently, cut into a player's confidence.

First, check to see if you are overswinging—trying to get your club back as far as you do on your woods. If you find you are, shorten your backswing. When you are hitting the ball on the target again, then you can lengthen your backswing a bit at a time, and distance will come.

Second, if you are pulling your long irons, check your finish. Perhaps you haven't allowed your weight to move over to the left leg. Holding your weight back on the right will cause a pull. Taking your club back too much on the inside also does.

And third, if you're pushing your long irons off to the right, you should again check your finish. You are probably quitting or not following through all the way. Make sure that your clubhead is finishing over your left shoulder. If that is in order, then check your backswing to see that the club is not being taken back too far on the outside.

Correct

Incorrect: Player has blocked
follow-through. Push will result

Incorrect: Player has not moved
weight to left leg. Pull will result

139

68

CARY MIDDLECOFF

U. S. Open Champion, 1949 and 1956

The Punch Shot

I want to give you a safety-first shot. It's called the punch shot, and you can play it from the 3-iron up to the 9. When properly hit, a punch shot flies in a low trajectory. It never "takes off" on you like a high-flying approach. It sits down with a little drag on it when it lands, and recommends itself as an especially fine control shot to play when you have a following wind and there is lots of trouble back of the green. I use it regularly when I want to be certain to avoid going over a green and collecting extra strokes for my troubles.

Let's say I have an approach of 160 yards. I could get there with a 6-iron, but instead I take a 5. One club more is the general rule. I grip the club slightly lower down the shaft and play the ball a bit closer to my right foot. I close the face of the club —just a fraction—and I drag it back more than usual. I use a three-quarters length swing. As I come down, my hands are farther in front than they normally are and I don't uncock quite so fast. This delay in the snap gives the feel of punching at the ball, and this action gives the ball the flight and the drag that keeps it from going farther than the player intends.

Cary Middlecoff's hands are well ahead as he comes into the ball on the punch shot

69

TOMMY BOLT
U. S. Open Champion, 1958

Technique for the Middle Irons

The five-iron is one of my favorite clubs because, of all the sticks, it seems to be the most natural utility club. If you want to hit it a little lower, you just move the ball back. If you want to hit it a little higher, you move it up a bit. You do the same with all the clubs to modify the flight of your shots, of course, but the five, maybe because it is the middle iron, somehow hits me as most adaptable for playing particular golf shots particular ways. Ordinarily I play the five with the ball in the center of my stance and I try to cut across the ball just a shade from left to right. You tend to pull across the ball if you try to come into it dead square.

When I'm playing the five and the other middle irons, the main thing I concentrate on is swinging with an even tempo, letting the club head do the job and not trying to increase the tempo and speed of my swing just before impact. Most of the 80- and 90-golfers I see forget all about tempo with the middle irons. This accounts for the fact that for every green they hit with these clubs, they hit six or seven approaches into the traps either on the left or right of the green. Granted that the average golfer can't wait for the club head as long as a pro can, but he can wait longer than he thinks he can. If he works on waiting just that split second longer, rather than powering the ball and getting the shot over with, he'll play better shots because he has to use the club head if he waits on it. So wait on it, men.

143

70

DOW FINSTERWALD

PGA Champion, 1958

Playing the Middle Irons

The straighter the face of the club, the more difficult it is to play. Even though this is true, it is not true to the extent most people think. In more specific language, what I'm trying to get across is this: granted that it *is* easier for the average golfer to hit a good shot with his eight-iron than it is with his four-iron, he will obtain much better results than he usually does with the middle irons if he goes about playing them right.

You can play the short irons with a restricted swing and just hit down on the ball, and sometimes get away with it. That won't work in the middle irons—the lowest point of the arc of the swing is not so far in advance of the ball as on the shorter irons. You must execute a golf swing. On the middle irons you don't have to hit the ball with a lot of force to get it out the distance you want. The club will do it for you if you perform a reasonably good swing. The backswing should be almost as full as the backswing on the long irons and the woods. This necessarily means taking a good unrestricted body turn.

As compared with the short irons, the longer turn you make in playing the middle irons provides more club head speed for you. There's more acceleration of the hands through the ball. There's no need to try to speed up your tempo. As a matter of fact, a golfer is wise if he tries to keep the same tempo on all his shots and realizes that he derives his distance not from speeding up his swing but from the built-in acceleration that the longer turn generates.

144

Incorrect   Correct

71

JACK BURKE, JR.

Masters Champion, 1956

Hit That Cloud!

My experience, as a now fairly veteran tournament player, has brought home to me that, regardless of some minor things I may or may not be doing on a given round, my game will be fundamentally sound if I stay under the shot.

To explain this a bit: there is always a tendency when you are aiming for a pin situated on the same level with yourself, to try and line the ball on a low, bullet-like flight for the target. When you have this conception in your mind of the shot you're going to play, you're likely to overaccelerate the whole action at contact and to hammer the ball so that it slides to the right, ducks a little to the left—or, at any rate, does something erratic.

When I find I'm doing this—and, I hope, sometimes before an error informs me—I try to remind myself that a shot that flies in a high trajectory seldom goes crooked. Instead of setting my eyes on the pin, I raise them and pick out some higher object behind the pin as my target—the top of a tree, a spot on a slope, or even a cloud. Then, by swinging in such a way that my shot will soar toward that object, I will move into the ball with an action that encourages staying under the shot. I am convinced that there's tremendous value in keeping this image, this precept, always in the forefront of my mind.

72

CARY MIDDLECOFF

U. S. Open Champion, 1949 and 1956

Hitting the Green

The one word that I think best describes the faults of the average golfer is *overextending*. If there is a secret to golf, it is to know one's capabilities. My advice is never to overextend even if a particular hole or situation seems completely hopeless. Play within yourself, and you will be surprised how often the cup seems to come to you.

Let us say you have a fairly long approach shot. Nine times out of ten, you are much better off playing for the middle of the green instead of for the flag. Whenever you sit down after a round and review it hole by hole, you will find that when you went for the flag, you usually missed the green entirely or ended up in a sand trap. How much wiser to give yourself a larger target to hit: the whole green. And really, even on that exceptional occasion when you play a fairly long approach right on the line to the pin, what do you gain? Generally, you still end up just about as many feet from the cup as you do when you succeed in hitting the area around the center of the green. Concentrate on hitting *the green*. The cup will come to you.

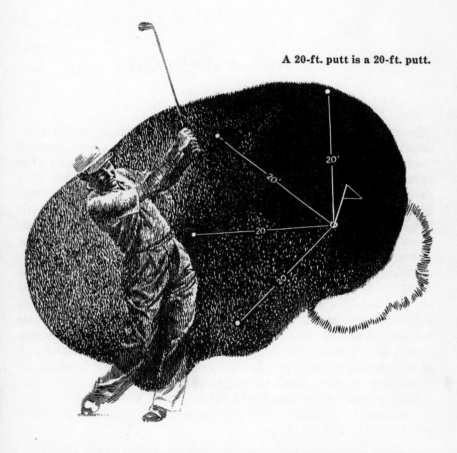

A 20-ft. putt is a 20-ft. putt.

Putts are no longer from the center of the green than from a point on a line of the "perfect approach." They are no harder to hole

73

TOMMY ARMOUR

U. S. Open Champion, 1927

The Active Right Side

Playing in a tournament at Pinehurst at one time, I had a very comfortable lead going into the last nine holes. I was playing very well when suddenly my iron shots started to spray. I was hitting the ball in the center of the club and the flight was correct, but the ball would veer just far enough to the right to land in the bunkers. This happened at the 10th, 11th, 12th and 13th holes and cost me a stroke each hole. Although I had a good lead, I could not afford to throw it away at that pace. The funny thing about it was that I did not know what I was doing.

Going down the 14th, a very difficult par four, Phil Perkins came up to me and said, "Tommy, your right side is stuck." Of course, anyone who plays golf knows that this can be disastrous. I had hit an adequate drive on the 14th. Before playing my second shot, I thought of what Phil had told me and I took a couple of practice swings allowing my right side to come in. I then knocked my second shot straight on the pin and continued to hit fine straight irons on the remaining holes.

I have never forgotten Phil's tip—I would never have won the tournament without it—and I suggest most emphatically that you try to remember it.

Incorrect position at the finish of the swing (below) shows that the player's right side has not come into the shot at all. Correct positions (right, upper and lower) illustrate the full pivot of the hips and shoulders at the top of the backswing and at the conclusion of the stroke

74

JULIUS BOROS

U. S. Open Champion, 1952

Achieving Backspin

Golfers seem to have two ambitions above all others: they would like to be able to drive as long as the pros and to be able to stop their approaches on the greens the way the pros can. Much sensible instruction has been provided on how to gain length off the tee, but it has been my experience that the average golfer is quite confused on the business of backspin.

First, let me tell you how, contrary to popular belief, one does not achieve backspin: you don't get it by over-emphasizing the down motion of the downswing—that is, by simply driving the ball into the ground as forcefully as you can.

Backspin, to some degree, depends on the relationship of the power of the blade to the power of the shaft. You must have the right equipment first. Then—it is all very unmysterious and painstaking—backspin is produced by contacting the ball absolutely cleanly, striking it a quarter of an inch or so above its base as you hit down-and-through the ball. This takes plenty of time and some skill to master, but it is this precise striking of the ball that creates the spin in flight that in turn creates the backspin action when the ball hits the green.

The "secret" of the backspin lies in striking the ball cleanly and accurately

75

AL MENGERT

Echo Lake CC, Westfield, N. J.

Swinging the Pitch Shot

The secret of scoring on the pro tour is getting down in two shots when you're about a hundred yards from the green. The average club golfer has more modest demands. He doesn't expect to get down in a pitch and a putt very often, but he would like to be able to pitch well enough so that he has a crack at a one-putt green every now and then and can at least count on regularly hitting the green with his pitch. He doesn't always do that, you know. A good many times when he scoops his shot the ball lands short and expires on the apron. Other times, when he tries to put a little punch into his shot, he pulls or pushes it far off the line. These particular errors are hard for him to take because the pitch shot doesn't require a full and powerful swing, as driving does or true finesse, as trouble shots do. The pitch is one shot he thinks he ought to be able to handle pretty well.

I believe in learning a standard pitch that is a swinging stroke as opposed to a slapping hit. The concept the player should have is that this shot is quite similar to the way you toss a ball underhand: just direct the right arm and hand toward the target. On the short pitch there's no body turn to speak of—you use your left side far less than you do on a full swing. As for your right arm and hand, you shouldn't think of them until you're coming down into the ball. Then they swing through the ball together and go right on out toward the target. There isn't an easier shot to learn or a more reliable one.

76

BOB WATSON
Fairview CC, Elmsford, N. Y.

Developing Touch and Control

Golfers tend to confuse touch with control. They use the two words as though they were interchangeable, which, of course, they are not. Unless you have touch, or feel, as it is sometimes called, you cannot have control. That is the kernel of it.

I was lucky enough to have started playing golf when I was young, and learned the feel of golf shots then. A group of us kids would go out and play a triangle of holes with just one club. We would do everything with it—hit the ball high and low, run shots or stop them with backspin. The next time out we would do the same thing with another club. We didn't realize it then, but we were getting a marvelous education in the uses of clubs. People learning to play today generally are equipped with a club for each distinct shot. They hit the ball full each time, but that is the trouble with their game. They can only hit the ball full.

To acquire touch, I advise that you go back to where I began and practice playing with a single club. You can play several holes with the club. Or you might try the practice fairway. Select a target down the fairway—say 50 to 125 yards away. Then hit balls at it until you feel you have mastered the club. You might try a long iron at first. Go to a higher iron after that. You will find as you go through the irons that you will have to do a lot of gripping up and down the shaft, that you will be opening and closing your stance and lengthening and shortening your swing. Eventually you will find yourself instinctively hitting balls with the right spin and height and length. These are the elements of control.

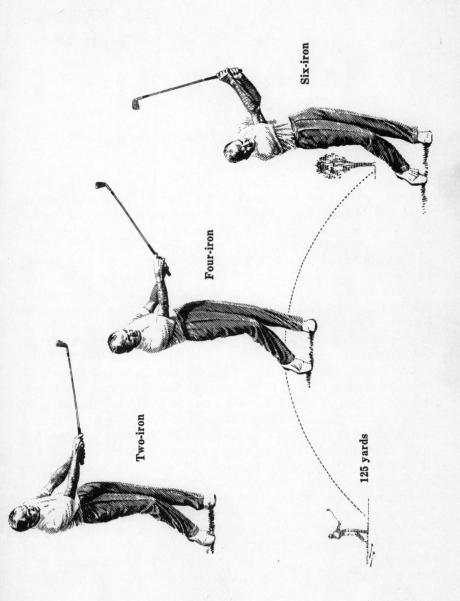

Six-iron

Four-iron

Two-iron

125 yards

Part IV
Getting Out of Trouble

77

JOE PRYKE

Gorge Vale Golf Club, Victoria, B. C.

Hooding the Wedge in the Rough

The club that has done the most to revolutionize golf in the last 25 years is the wedge. At the same time it seems to have been more of a boon for the accomplished players than it has for the poorer players for whom it was supposed to eliminate a lot of trouble, too. For instance, it was said that the wedge would make it easier for average golfers to get out of the rough, but as often as not they would be just as well off going with the old niblick or nine-iron. It is the extra weight in the head of the wedge that seems to throw less expert golfers off. They have difficulty getting the club head through the shot without the face opening on them.

When you are playing out of the rough you can help the wedge to do its stuff if you hood the face, or turn the toe in slightly. This minor change in the head's position will counteract the resistance of the tall grass. It seems to streamline the head more, and the face goes right through without opening. This hooding helps women players especially, for they don't have the same strength men do in forcing the heavy club through whatever is growing around the ball in the rough.

It takes a little practice and it looks wrong to the eye at first, but hooding the face of the wedge also facilitates recovering from traps where the sand is loose. You should also know that hooding the wedge on those 25-to-50-yard pitches from the fairway will send your ball in low with a good deal of check or bite on it.

Club face open

Club face hooded

78

WALTER BURKEMO

PGA Champion, 1953

The Long Trap Shot

When the average golfer gets into a sand trap 75 yards or so from the green, he wants to play an explosion shot "like the pros." He takes in the healthy distance to the green and says to himself, "Now I'll really have to blast it to get it there." The results don't help his frame of mind much, or his score either.

To begin with, the average golfer is wrong when he thinks the pros play an explosion shot from that far out. The clubhead, of course, sometimes displaces quite a bit of sand *after* the ball has been struck, and maybe this is what gives the illusion that the pros hit the sand before the ball on this kind of shot. They don't —or at least they try not to. They try to "pick" the ball on a long trap shot, contacting it cleanly and hitting it just below the center.

On this shot there's very little shifting of weight. You keep the body anchored, for you play this shot just about entirely with the arms and wrists. You have to cock the wrists correctly going back to execute the shot well. And you must concentrate, for no shot in which the club has to make precise contact with the ball is an easy one. One further point: always use the sand wedge.

79

AL ESPOSITO

Country Club of Charleston, S. C.

Pitching from Sandy Rough

On seaside and desert courses particularly, but wherever sand exists, golfers run into a shot that few of them can cope with successfully. This is a short, lofted pitch from the sandy rough that must carry over a nearby embankment to reach the green. The object, obviously, is to get the ball up and over the embankment without punching it with so much forward drive that it either carries or rolls on over the green—where, of course, a nice little trap is usually lying in wait. In his consternation when he finds himself beset with this shot, the average golfer does little more than try to get the shot over with.

If the golfer will keep calm and regard this shot as a cousin of the explosion shot—which it primarily is—he will find he can deal with it without much trouble. Use your wedge, with your feet together and your hands a shade forward. Take the club back a little on the outside, with the left hand in charge. Hit the sand about an inch behind the ball. Don't let the hands roll over as you go through the ball. Keep the back of the left hand pointing up toward the sky on the follow-through. The ball should come up arching high and should fall without too much forward roll.

Play the lie in sandy rough
as an explosion shot

80

JOHNNY REVOLTA

PGA Champion, 1935

The Fundamental Explosion Shot

It doesn't happen very often but every now and then you hear reports that this or that professional purposely played his approach shot to a treacherous green into a greenside trap—in order to be certain of getting down in two shots. I mention this not because it is a strategy I would recommend, but it does serve to emphasize how confident most pros feel about trap shots. For the average golfer, on the other hand, this is the shot he fears most of all. He plays it with a wavering mind and trembling hand. He muffs it, and so it remains the shot he fears the most.

When you are exploding from loose sand, you must play a very firm stroke with a purposeful follow-through. Your wedge should enter the sand about an inch behind the ball. It should drive through the sand in a straight furrow some six inches long. Or to put it another way, the club head continues to plow through the sand for five inches or so past the spot where the ball lay. If you stay down over the shot and concentrate on plowing a straight furrow, I can assure you that you will soon be on your way to becoming a confident trap player.

Johnny Revolta demonstrates the furrow technique for playing the explosion shot

81

HELEN DETTWEILER

Thunderbird CC, Palm Springs, Calif.

Lazy Does It in the Trap Shot

Nine times out of 10 when a player finds his or her ball lying in a sand trap, the reaction is one of great trepidation. Women are particularly susceptible to this, and they approach the trap shot with such a mixture of hopelessness and fear that, on numerous occasions, they waste two or three heedless, headless strokes before they even calm down.

Actually, as has been said time and time again, the trap shot is about the easiest in golf, *if you take it easy*. Remember, you do not have to slug the ball with all your might to get it out of the trap. All it takes is a good, coordinated swing. Since the club enters the sand behind the ball and has to travel beneath the top of the sand, a full swing with a complete follow-through is necessary. This is what you should aim for, not a frenzied slash which, most likely, will only bury the club and the ball deep in the sand.

The big secret in playing from sand is to be lazy about it. Take the club back with a slight wrist break and raise the club a little more abruptly, and remember that the last thing you want to do is to get savage with the shot. The ball will come floating out of the trap much more successfully, be assured, if you put your mind to executing a swing that is unrushed and easy-flowing from its start to the finish of a complete follow-through.

Incorrect: overtense

Correct: lazy does it

169

82

PHIL TAYLOR

Victoria Golf Club, Victoria, B. C.

Playing from Hard and Soft Sand

Wedge shots, whether from hard sand or soft must not be forced. They must be played with an easy, lazy swing in which the sand is used as a buffer to *poofff* the ball out. And, of course, to get results you must follow through and complete your arc.

If you are in a trap where the sand is reasonably soft, aim to hit a spot about two inches behind the ball. The wedge will do the rest.

If the sand is hard or wet, you cannot hit so far behind the ball, because the packed sand will offer too much resistance and your wedge won't be able to travel through the sand beneath the ball as it must. In these conditions, you should aim at a spot about an inch or so behind the ball. Swing the club a little more upright and use a shorter swing and follow-through. You may have to use a little more power than when you are playing from soft sand but not much more. Keep your swing essentially lazy.

Now, if you have a bad lie, say, a lie in a footprint, you've got to waive the no-power rule and hit this one hard. You aim at a spot just behind the ball, use an upright swing with no pivot and hit forcefully—as if you were trying to bury the clubhead in the sand beneath the ball.

Soft sand

Hard sand

83

FRED NOVAK

St. Andrews Golf Club, Hastings-on-Hudson, N. Y.

Open Stance on Bunker Shots

Compare the way a good player and a mediocre one handle their sand shots, and you will see quite a difference. So often, when I am playing a round with members who score in the 90s, a player who misplays his first shot in a bunker will go on and miss his next four or five bunker shots. If weekend golfers would learn how to blast the ball out of a trap, there is no knowing the amount of grief and the number of strokes they would save themselves.

Their trouble begins when they position themselves in a bunker as if they were going to hit a fairway shot. In a sand trap a square stance is ruinous. It encourages taking the club back too much on the inside, and it leads the player into a bigger pivot than the shot calls for. He comes into the ball with too flat a swing. As a result, he generally lines the ball well over the green or, in an attempt to avoid this extreme error, he purposely babies the shot and often doesn't manage to get the ball out of the hazard.

In a bunker it is best to use an open stance, advancing the right foot four or five inches nearer the ball than the left. The stance restricts the pivot and assists the player in taking the club straight up and straight down. This is what the shot calls for. It is strictly a firm left-arm shot. You don't sweep the ball out of a bunker. You want to take your wedge straight up and then straight down, a little outside-in if anything. Then you want to spank the sand an inch or a little more behind the ball. It is the sand that ejects the ball.

Incorrect

Correct

173

84

BETTY JAMESON

San Antonio Country Club, San Antonio, Texas

Securing the Stance in Traps

Golfers who customarily take pains to obtain a firm, correct stance before hitting their shots go to sleep frequently in this department when confronted with recovering from a bunker. I have in mind those times when the ball lies within the concave dip of a bunker in such a position that the player must stand a few inches above it or below it.

Although there isn't much that a player can do about his stance if the ball lies *above* him—aside from making sure that he is properly balanced—he can greatly enhance his chances of a good shot when the ball lies *below* him if he will shovel his feet into the sand until they are down to the same level as the ball. He can then move into hitting the shot without "dropping" his swing inches below its normal plane in order to make the desired contact with the ball or the sand behind the ball.

The next time you are faced with this predicament, simply take your regular stance. Then, as you line yourself up and soak in the shot generally, squidge your heels back and forth in the sand until your feet and the ball are resting on the same level. You will probably play better trap shots; and really you should, since you've made the shot an appreciably easier one.

Preparatory stance   **Feet shoveled in**

85

AL ESPOSITO

Country Club of Charleston, S. C.

Bankside Lies

One shot many golfers have a misconception about is the recovery from an uphill bank in the rough that fringes the green area. It is really quite a simple shot. In taking your stance—which is the key to making the shot simple—the golfer should bend his left knee to compensate for the incline of the slope and should play the ball just slightly forward of the center of his body. The right shoulder should be down a bit, but the incline usually takes care of that anyhow.

The golfer should step up to this shot understanding that it is a member of the chip-shot family. The common error golfers make is to pick the club up steeply on the backswing and to force the hands quickly up and over on the follow-through, as though all the stroke required were a punch-scoop delivered with all possible strength. What this faulty technique accomplishes is to drive the ball into the bank. Instead, the golfer should understand that he is playing the stroke correctly when there is only slight wrist-break action and when the back of his left hand goes straight out toward the pin, as it does on an ordinary chip. The club head should stay low, merely following the upslope of the bank. The angle of the club face provides all the loft that is needed. It is up to the golfer to provide the delicacy the shot calls for.

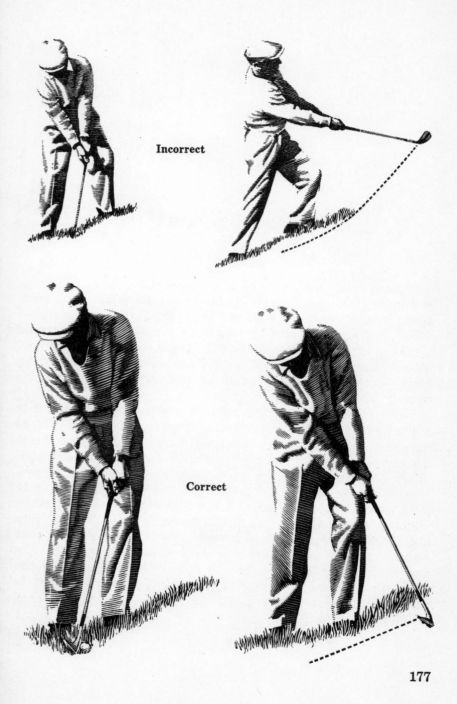

Incorrect

Correct

177

Part V
On and Around the Green

86

WALLY GRANT

Mt. Lebanon Golf Club, Pittsburgh

The Short Pitch

Pitch shots from 10 to 50 yards out are easier to execute if you play the ball center instead of off the right foot. Most beginners, when attempting to play this shot from the right foot, will invariably keep their weight back on the right side throughout the stroke, flapping their hands up at the ball instead of hitting through the ball.

I tell beginners to lean laterally against the left foot when they address a pitch shot. Then they will be in a hitting position right from the start. They should stay in that position, rather than attempt to move the weight to the right and then back to the left leg during the swing for, as we all realize, very little body action is used on a pitch shot.

The main thing to work for on the pitch is keeping the club face square as long as you can as you whip it through the ball. I find it helps many of my pupils if they alter their grip a little so that the V of the left-hand grip points to the chin rather than to the right shoulder, as is orthodox on the full swing. In any event, when you are practicing your short pitches, work on swinging the club face straight through the ball for at least seven or eight inches past impact. That's the action you want.

Incorrect

Correct

181

87

JIMMY D'ANGELO

Dunes Golf and Beach Club, Myrtle Beach, S. C.

Lobbing the Pitch

A short approach to a fast green guarded by traps presents an interesting challenge with rewarding satisfactions. To hold the green by means of backspin (developed by punching the ball into the turf) requires considerable practice and skill, possibly more than the average golfer can bring to his occasional rounds. Accordingly, it's a wise decision for golfers to cultivate the lob type of approach, a shot which reduces the percentage of error and which does the job very well, too. When correctly executed, the lobbed pitch sends the ball up to the green in a very steep trajectory. The ball drops almost vertically onto the green, and little roll results.

In playing this shot, use a nine-iron or a pitching wedge. Take your stance with the ball an inch or so farther forward than usual. Allow yourself a backswing somewhat longer than you would use if you were planning to spank a backspin approach the same distance and allow your wrists to cock freely. Swing smoothly and well through the ball. You will find that the ball will get up very quickly and sit down very well when it plops onto the green.

This shot can be easily learned with a little practice and can be just as effective as the much more exacting backspin shot.

The ball is played slightly
farther forward than usual

In following through, do not
whip the club around but let
it go out toward the hole

Allow yourself a
liberal backswing

88

MARLENE BAUER HAGGE

Delray Beach, Fla.

The Short Lofted Pitch

Contrary to the popular notion, most of the pros don't use much wrist cock in playing their short pitches. For myself, though, I find I hit the ball sharpest and control it best if I use lots of wrist and hand action on this type of shot, with the hands completely uncocked at impact. I play the ball two inches forward of the right heel. This requires "early timing," and a golfer probably is best off to start by playing this shot off the middle and then to move the ball back when his (or her) timing develops. My reason for advocating this method is this: the lowest part of the swing occurs at the center of the stance; in order to hit the ball first, the turf after, you have to place the ball back.

In lining up the short pitch, I lay the blade open, very slightly. I stand with my left shoulder held high, so that it is free to do its work. (I also have the feeling that my left elbow is high at address.) I start the club back with my left shoulder and arm, and halfway through the backswing I begin cocking my wrists. On this shot I allow for a little roll. For example, on a 40-yard pitch I try to gauge the shot so that the ball will land about 12 feet short of the hole.

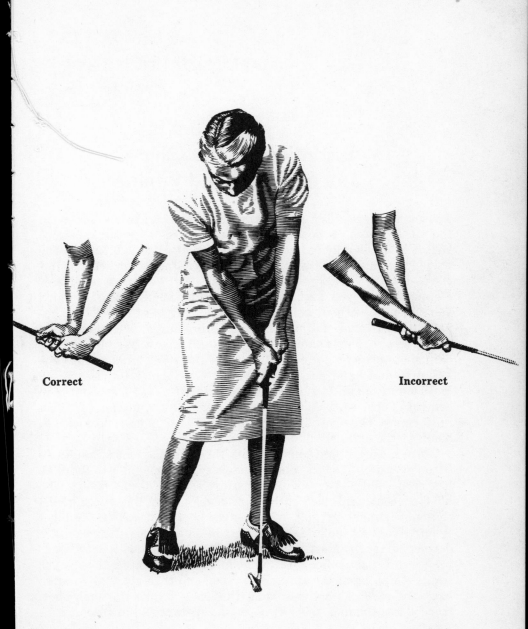

Correct   Incorrect

185

89

LEW MYERS

Ledgemont CC, Seekonk, Mass.

Essentials of the Chip

Too many players try to push or scoop the ball to the green on their chip shots. A good chip is a much freer stroke. It begins with the application of certain fundamentals we all know—the blade kept square to the line, the club head never picked up. But the essence of it is the stroke. You can never become a consistent chipper unless you first develop a sound, efficient stroke which you can play without being conscious of hitting the ball. On impact, the left arm and hand should be in charge. The right joins in the stroke, but it shouldn't dominate it, the way it does in the chip shots of poor golfers. With them the right hand pushes the left arm and hand out of the way, which brings on inaccuracy and lack of touch. It is quite the reverse when the left hand is in control. Then, regardless of the club you use, you can count on uniformity. The shot is always on line. There is no conscious collision of the ball and club head at impact.

Since most golfers don't possess the muscular coordination to become scratch players, and since every golfer wants to score as low as possible, at every club there is a handful of players who have concentrated with success on developing a fine short game, that department of golf which saves so many strokes and yet requires less muscular talent than full shots. These players have developed touch. Most golfers can do the same with intelligent practice. I particularly recommend sessions where the player begins chipping at the apron of a green and then gradually moves back, 10 yards at a time, using the same stroke for each shot, merely lengthening the swing as the distance requires.

The left arm and hand are in control
going back and on the forward stroke

187

90

JOHNNY REVOLTA

PGA Champion, 1935

Hitting Down on the Chip

When it comes to chip shots, it seems that practically every golfer has an inborn fear he won't give the ball enough loft. He wants to see that ball travel in a high arc, so he sets his weight back on the right leg and makes a jerky swing with his hands back of the club head at the moment of impact. The result is that he not only opens the club face too much but he also pulls his body upward in his convulsive scooping motion. Instead of lifting the ball in a crisp arc, he is lucky if he doesn't hit way behind it or skull it over the green.

To correct these faults, first make sure your left wrist is straight and on a line with the shaft. Then, when you swing, the key thing to remember is the hands, not the wrists. The backswing uses both hands evenly, with a certain amount of play in the wrists. So does the downswing. *The hands lead the club head slightly.* At impact you should feel yourself striking down and through the ball. This action may at first give you the sensation that you are closing the club head, but actually you are just giving yourself a chance to follow through in a straight line that follows the course of the ball. The loft of the club head will supply all the loft you need.

Correct position at address, hands in front of the ball

Incorrect position for playing a chip shot

The club head follows through on straight line to the target

91

JOHNNY PALMER

Tulsa Country Club

The Chip and Run

In recent years I've noticed that a great many golfers take their wedge or their 9-iron to play almost all their shots from off the edge of the green. There are times, of course, when the shot you should play, or must play, is a lofted little pitch calculated to drop near the pin and expire there with as little run as you can manage. But there are many more times—particularly when the pin lies to the rear of the green and there is a lot of room between your ball and the pin—when the most efficient and reliable shot to play is the good old chip-and-run. You just calculate how far you want to hit the ball in the air so that, after landing, it will have the legs to roll right up to the stick. You can't go very wrong with this shot.

You can play this run-up with any iron from the four through the nine, depending on your lie, the speed and the contours of the green, and your personal taste. To play this shot well and consistently well, you must learn to pace your swing just as you do on a regular shot, for the club head has to get in there with the same timing as on a full swing. Contact the ball and the turf at almost the same time, taking just that little amount of turf that gives you the sense of making contact with it. You will get some bite on this shot if you play it right, for bite comes from precise timing and precise impact and not, as most golfers think, from jabbing the ball down.

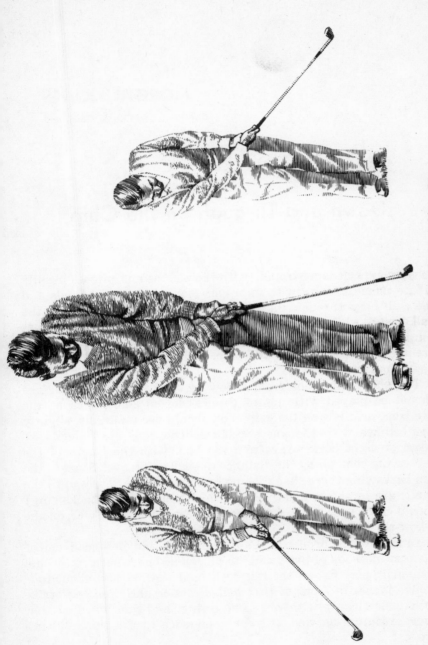

Johnny Palmer demonstrates the correct technique for the chip-and-run

92

MORGAN JONES

California Golf Course, Cincinnati

Down and Through on the Chip

Players experiencing trouble with their chips and pitches usually create their difficulty with improper movement of the hands and the club head through the ball. The club head must contact the ball crisply while moving down and through the ball. This is just the reverse of the ineffectual flip which results when the hands are allowed to slow down and stop, and the wrists break sharply up at impact.

The short chip shot from a few feet off the putting surface should be played with one of the less lofted clubs, such as the five-iron, held low on the grip. You should use a narrow, slightly open stance with the knees relaxed. The club head should be taken straight back away from the ball, with the length of the backswing controlling the distance the ball will travel. Since in the full backswing there should be no breaking of the wrists until the hands are hip-high, a chip shot (which requires less backswing) should have very little wrist break either going back or on the follow-through.

To achieve the proper action of the hands and club head, one of the best methods of practice is to place one ball where you would ordinarily play it—off the left heel—and another ball about four or five inches in front of that ball. Practice until you can strike both balls cleanly with the same swing, and you will find that your execution as well as your confidence in the shot will improve.

Incorrect: the flip

Correct: down and through

193

93

SAM SNEAD

Masters Champion, 1949, 1952, and 1954

Chipping from the Fringe

The scoring in golf, as everyone knows, is done around the green. Even our finest golfers don't hit all the greens—a number of our top-circuit scorers miss quite a few—but they can get down in two from off the edge just like clockwork. Some over-90-shooters I've played with score that low only because they're pretty proey around the green, but the average over-90-shooter loses many savable strokes because he doesn't understand how to play a chip. This is one so-called simple shot that is really a simple shot. The average player, though, thinks he has to pitch the ball up in the air. He uses too lofted a club. He overpivots—transfers his weight too much—and swings so fast he can't get his weight back to the ball quick enough. As a result, he looks up, he fluffs, he scalps, he does everything.

Treat the chip from the fringe as a long putt. From a foot off the edge to fifteen or so feet off, don't take too lofted a club. Stand with your feet close together. Get your weight a bit on your left side and keep it there. Forget about lofting the ball, and play a brief, crisp little running stroke, relying on your sense of distance to tell you how hard to hit the shot, just as you would on a long approach putt.

The feet are close together, the weight slightly on left side, on the chip from the fringe

94

ART WALL, JR.

Masters Champion, 1959

The Short Chip from the Apron

When they are faced with a short chip from the apron of a green, most players feel compelled to try to loft the ball up to the pin. Their thinking here seems to be that every shot in golf, except the putt, has to travel through the air in a high arc and land right at the target. The result is that a great many golfers either use too lofted a club from the edge of the green or they make an even more serious mistake: they try to scoop the ball up— with faulty wrist action, of course.

Actually, the shot to play from the edge is a run-up—the kind of shot where the ball is hit a short distance in the air and then gradually sits down and rolls the rest of the way to the cup, as a putt does. The club to use is one of the middle irons—from the four-iron through the seven-iron, depending on the terrain and your own choice of clubs. (I generally go with the six-iron.)

To play a chip-and-run shot, the player must hit the ball first, the turf afterward. To do this, he must be sure and keep his wrists firm and to address the ball with his hands slightly ahead of the ball. The feet should be no more than 10 inches apart, the stance slightly open. With this unspectacular but sound method, you won't be leaving yourself eight- and 10-footers to hole. After a while you'll have five-footers or less.

There should be only the faintest suggestion
of wrist-break in the chip from off the edge

95

BILLY MAXWELL

Odessa CC, Odessa, Texas

Putting from Off the Edge

Whenever the contours of the green area make it possible to putt from off the green and the aprons are cut so that the ball will roll accurately over them, I use my putter as often as I can instead of chipping. I realize that in the book of high-style playing the "Texas wedge"—that's putting off the green—is still frowned upon, but it really is a great stroke-saver. I sometimes putt from as much as 10 or 20 feet off the green, and unless the apron grass prohibits it by being too high or rough, I almost always use my putter when I'm three or four feet off the putting surface.

I've probably had a little more experience than most golfers putting from off the green, growing up as I did in Odessa in Texas. The point is to use exactly the same technique as you would on the green. The gauging takes a little practice, but otherwise it's the same stroke as an approach putt. The main misconception people have is that they think they have to hit the ball from off the green, a little bit harder than is really necessary. When they try to give it that extra clip they come off the ball. Sometimes, both consciously and unconsciously, they tip the face of the putter back to give it the loft of a four-iron. Now, when you tip the blade back or simply hit the ball too hard, that makes the ball jump and bounce off the ground and lose its line. Use your normal stroke. That will keep the ball running true over the apron to the putting surface. You'll be up close regularly, I assure you, and, what is more, you can "miss" a shot when you're putting from off the green from long distances and still get the ball within five or six feet of the cup.

When putting from off the edge use the same technique as you would on the green

96

GENE SARAZEN
U. S. Open Champion, 1922 and 1932

The After-Forty Finger

The basic principle of good putting is to keep the blade of the putter square to the hole. When you talk turkey with a businessman, you must look squarely at him during the entire conversation. It's the same in putting. When you're talking turkey on the greens, the face of your putter must look squarely at the hole throughout the stroke.

Most of the time, when a golfer fails to take the putter back square to the target, the error he makes is "breaking" his wrists. This causes him to pull the putter off the line and eventually to cut the putt off to the right or yank it to the left of the hole.

To correct this habit of breaking the wrists, I suggest placing the index finger of the right hand so that it extends directly down the shaft—behind the shaft.

You can't break your wrists then, and the finger also serves as a fine guide in making the stroke.

I call this the "after-40 finger," since it has been especially helpful in improving the putting of my friends who are getting along in years, but I recommended it to golfers of all ages who are erratic on the green.

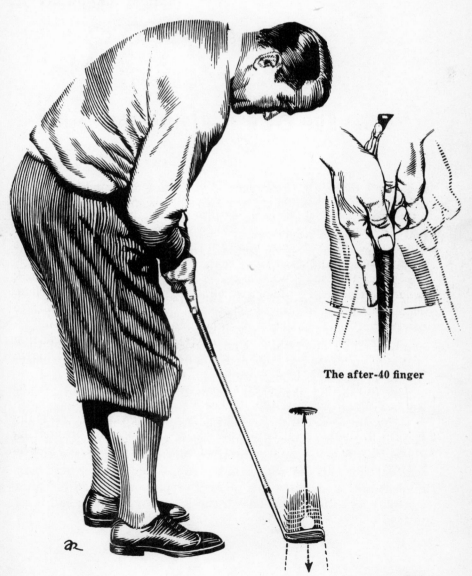

The after-40 finger

97

CHICK HARBERT

PGA Champion, 1954

The Eye Over the Ball in Putting

It doesn't make any difference if you have an unorthodox grip or stance when you putt, but two things are vital: your eye must be directly over the ball, and you must stroke the ball to make it rotate end-over-end.

You have undoubtedly noticed that manufacturers are now making putters more upright. This is to help the golfer keep his eye directly over the ball. Every great putter I have seen does this. In effect, their eyes act in the capacity of eyes for the ball. The ball can only "see" the line when your eyes are directly over it. If they are not, your eyes will see one line while the ball "sees" another, and I don't think I need to go into the results of that.

When your eyes are over the ball, you have a much better chance of stroking it accurately and imparting end-over-end-rotation. End-over-end rotation means that the ball is contacted so squarely that it rolls "over itself," on the same vertical axis, there being no side-spin as there inevitably will be when the ball is cut or pulled or mis-putted in some other manner. If a putt stroked with end-over-end rotation hits a corner of the cup, it will not spin off and will usually drop. Bobby Locke, that magnificent putter, daubs a line of Mercurochrome around his practice putting balls so that he can check exactly how the ball is rotating.

End-over-end rotation

The eye is directly over the ball

98

HORTON SMITH

Masters Champion, 1934 and 1936

The Box Principle in Putting

Putting is the most precise and certainly the most fickle part of golf. Through the years I have concluded there is a strong relationship between the psychology, philosophy and mechanics of this so-called "other" game.

I cannot overstress the value of a consistent and confident attitude toward putting. You must be positive, decisive, trustful and patient: positive in that you think every putt can be holed; decisive in that you never doubt your plan once you have made up your mind; trustful in that you realize that through learning and practice you have grooved your mechanics; patient in that you recognize that you will make your fair share of putts in relation to your skill, touch and intelligent practice. As many putts are missed through mental errors as mechanical.

Yet, first, there must be a sound mechanical foundation. This is what can be taught; the rest must be sensed. The basic point of all putting fundamental is squareness. I call it the "box" principle. It means simply that the feet, hips, shoulders and hands must all be square to the putting line. The key is the hand position: the back of the left hand and the palm of the right must always face directly toward the hole. The principle holds true at every stage of the putting stroke. You can achieve the square feeling of the left hand leading the backstroke and the right hand hitting squarely at and through impact only when you have mastered the box principle.

The position of the hands as they should be throughout the swing is shown at left. The club head is as it should be throughout the stroke—square to the line of putt—is shown right.

205

99

AL BESSELINK

Grossinger, N. Y.

One Method of Putting

I used to be an in-and-outer on the greens, but I've been putting very well, I'd say, since adopting George Low's method. George is one of the greatest putters any of us have encountered, and since his method is simplicity itself, I'd like to pass it along to you.

The fact that underlies George's method is the necessity of keeping the face of the putter square to the hole (or to the point on a rolling green you are aiming at) throughout the stroke. The position of the left hand on the shaft is the key to achieving this. At address, with the club face square, the back of the left hand must set up so that it is absolutely square to the hole. When you take the club back, as the left wrist breaks, the back of the left hand remains square. On the forward stroke, you simply let the weight of the club head strike the ball, with the back of the left hand remaining square to the hole right through to the finish of the stroke. When the back of the left hand is square to the hole, the putter face is also square, because they are always at the same angle.

Let me point out again, since it is very important, that on the forward stroke you don't urge the blade on with a deliberate action of the hands. You just let the weight of the club head create its own speed. The ball will be struck true and will roll with perfect rotation. All in all, it's a method that enables you to keep your body motionless when you putt and, moreover, it develops touch.

206

The back of the left hand remains square to the line at
address, on the downswing and on the follow-through

100

LEW MYERS

Ledgemont Country Club, Seekonk, Mass.

Developing an Accurate Putting Stroke

There are many styles of putting in common use which are of un-questioned merit, each style suiting certain players admirably. For those golfers who are not good putters, however, I would like to recommend a stroke which has often been referred to as the pendulum stroke, since the club head moves in an arc resembling the swing of a pendulum and the weight of the club head produces the momentum of the stroke. In this method, the control resides in the last three fingers of the left hand. The left hand starts the club back and leads it through the stroke. The key to keeping the club head on a straight line as it comes through is the left elbow. It must go out straight toward the hole or, on a rolling green, straight toward the desired line of play. When it does, it prevents the right hand from taking over and pushing the ball, or the left hand from breaking in and pulling the ball off the line.

Whenever a beginner comes to me, I start him on the putting green with this stroke. Here he gets the feel of the club head and learns to take the club back and forward low along the ground. To help him keep the club face square to the line of play, I place a club or a rod parallel to the line of play. Before I let him putt a ball, I have him practice bringing the putter back and forth along the emphasized desired line.

Of course, with this or any other putting stroke, the head must remain absolutely still through impact. If it moves, it will destroy your stroke and your accuracy.

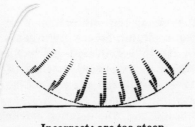

Incorrect: arc too steep

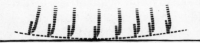

Correct: arc low along the ground

Practicing with ruler to develop the correct path for club head

101

TOMMY BOLT

U. S. Open Champion, 1958

Getting Behind the Putt

Putting styles vary from player to player. There's no reason why they shouldn't, for putting is a personal thing. In my own case, about a year and a half ago after a stretch of in-and-out work on the green, I adopted a slight change in my usual method of putting which did me a world of good. I altered my stance so that my body and arms were more behind the ball.

Getting more behind the putt enabled me to be much surer about many of the elements that make or break you on the green. It gave me a better line to the hole. It was much easier on my timing. I could hit the ball more solidly—right below the equator. To sum it up, this new position produced the picture in my mind that I could roll the ball smoothly and accurately toward the target, not unlike the way Buddy Bomar does in bowling.

When a player talks about rolling the ball toward the cup, I realize he is going against the present-day fashion which would have you rap the ball with a sharp, jabby hit. I don't think these pop strokes and bop strokes are here to stay. The game's top players could always stroke their putts, and that's the soundest method in the long run, I believe. In any event, getting behind the putt is easy for anyone to adapt to, and it has produced such good results for me that I recommend it to all golfers who are not natural tappers. You see that hole so much better.

102

A Lighter Right-Hand Putting Grip

I have become a steadier, more confident and an altogether better putter since I changed my putting grip not so long ago. Where my right hand used to be dominant, now my left hand is. I hold the club quite tightly in my left hand, with the hand well under the shaft. This brings firmness into the left wrist—firmness all the way up the left arm, in fact. And when you take the putter back, the left wrist doesn't break. It remains firm.

Since adopting this new grip and style, I am not conscious at all of the right hand during the stroke, but I certainly used to be. I was so tense with the right hand on the backstroke that I would pick the club up outside the line and would frequently hit the ball with the heel of the putter.

Employing this new left-hand control, I find I keep the putter blade close to the putting surface without having to make a deliberate effort to do this. Furthermore, the blade contacts the ball squarely. That, of course, is what makes a ball roll true. When I putted with the right hand in control, I used to flip the ball and it rolled so erratically that it never fell when it caught a corner of the cup. Now it seems the cup is a lot more receptive.

212

213

103

JOE PRYKE

Gorge Vale Golf Club, Victoria, B. C.

Contacting the Ball with the Putter

An important thing to remember when putting is the action of the ball itself. A ball that is struck in the center runs much truer than one struck below or above the center. The latter reacts to any irregularity of the green, but the ball hit amidships rolls over most green imperfections without losing its line.

With this in mind I advise my pupils to modify in their own minds the old rule to keep the putter as low to the ground as possible. If you put a ball down on your living room carpet or on a green and place one of today's narrow-bladed putters behind it, you will notice that the center of the ball is in line with the top of the blade. Consequently, when you putt, you should make a small adjustment in your stroke and concentrate on bringing the center of the blade through the center of the ball. When you make this kind of contact you'll hear that nice crisp sound all good putters produce.

On uphill putts I think you will find you'll get a helpfully strong overspin on the ball if you shut the face of putter slightly. Conversely, on downhill putts where delicacy is needed, the face of the putter is "turned uphill," or laid back just a shade.

214

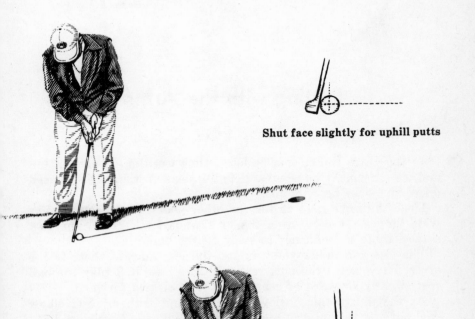

Shut face slightly for uphill putts

Open face for downhill putts

215

104

MARLENE BAUER HAGGE

Delray Beach, Fla.

Putting with the Arms

Over the years I have spent a lot of time working on my putting and, as a result, I have some definite ideas on the subject based on what works best for me.

I use the same grip as for the other shots. I advocate a very wide stance. It sets up a firmer foundation. With a narrow stance, there's a tendency to sway off the ball.

The less you break your wrists, the less margin there is for error. I try to hit the putt rather than stroke it. I play the ball just slightly forward of center—an inch or two forward.

As the illustrations below show, I stand with my left elbow well out and riding very high. My right elbow is kept close in to my right side; in that position it helpfully restricts me from taking the putter back too far. I start my stroke by pushing the left elbow back. This key movement of the elbow I can best describe by saying that the elbow moves the way it would if some imaginary hand were pushing it back.

I use this method because I feel that I can take the elbow (and the putter head) back on a very straight line from the ball. On the forward part of the putting stroke, I try to return the putter head to the same position it had at address.

The left elbow moves back as if some imaginary hand were pushing it

105

RALPH HUTCHISON

Saucon Valley Country Club, Bethlehem, Pa.

The Wrists Opposed in Putting

A high proportion of the best golfers today use the reverse overlap grip—the index finger of the left hand laps over the right and rides in the channel between the small finger and the third finger of the right hand. Regardless of what type of grip they use, all the best putters proceed on the principle of having the wrists opposed. That is, if you opened your hands, the palms would be facing each other.

With the wrists opposed, both thumbs are on top of the shaft. The left hand should be firm and, though it must not be tense, it should be on the side of tightness, not lightness. This grip has a tendency to put control of the stroking in the firm left hand, with most of the control exercised by the little finger and the two fingers adjoining it.

Gene Littler is a perfect illustration of a player who uses this opposed-wrists technique beautifully. He is a delight to watch because his entire style of putting is very sound and it is a style that all golfers, both men and women, can easily employ. To insure free and proper movements in his hands, Gene points his left elbow toward the hole and supports the right forearm slightly on the right thigh. He plays the ball in the center of his stance—normally his feet are about eight inches apart—which puts overspin on the ball and helps it hold its line. He keeps his eyes directly over the ball; his head remains still. He takes an ample backswing which permits the left elbow and hand to go forward and through with the stroke.

218

The reverse overlapping grip

Ralph Hutchison demonstrates how the wrists should be opposed to each other

106

MARY LENA FAULK

Glen Arven CC, Thomasville, Ga.

Recovering Your Putting Stroke

The essence of good putting—indeed, the essence of golf—is to hit the ball squarely. When you are doing this you get a great deal of the ball on the putter, a great feeling of the grass, a great feeling for distance.

All golfers, but tournament players perhaps more than the others, know the value of preserving a good putting stroke. Nevertheless, everyone, including the most gifted and conscientious golfers, loses his stroke at certain times. All the experienced players have their own methods of getting it back again. When I begin to lose the line or my firmness goes off on the green, I fall back on a relatively simple exercise to recover it. I like it because it is not too complicated and also because it gets you back on your stroke in such a way that it releases that fear of hitting the ball aggressively—which, as you know, can build up in a person who has been fighting a putting slump.

First, I take my left hand off the club and practice putting with my right hand only. Then I switch and putt with the left hand only. I find that when I putt with one hand I have to get set up more honestly to get my line and get the ball rolling. You cannot work the ball haphazardly and get away with anything at all— as you can when you putt with two hands.

Just one session on the practice green, practicing first with the right, then with the left and then with both hands, is quite often enough to set up again the right actions and a workably sound stroke.

220

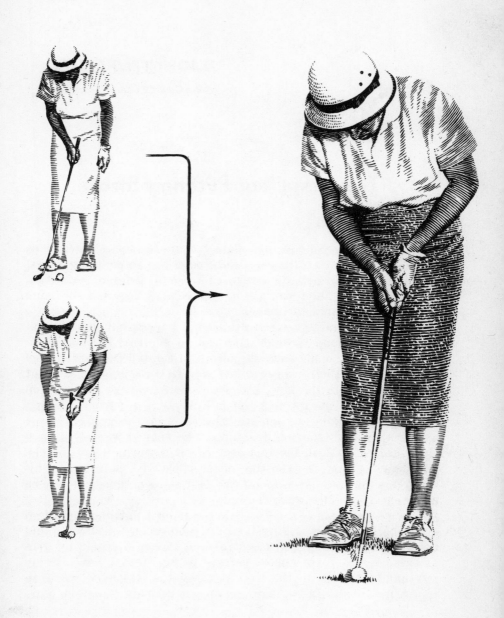

107

JOHNNY PALMER

Tulsa Country Club, Tulsa, Okla.

The Simplified Putting Stroke

When putting techniques are dissected and discussed, it strikes me that perhaps too little is said about the role timing plays. Granted that the putting stroke calls for a different execution from the tee-to-green strokes, nevertheless it requires the same sense of timing that the longer shots do.

In this day and age when people are happiest if you can reveal to them some "inside" shortcut to success, I realize how commonplace it must seem to golfers to remind them that they must work on their timing above all. Nevertheless, it is what puts the ball into the hole, and the various mannerisms the top putters employ simply help the individual to refine his timing. For myself, putting is, and has always been, the application of a few tried-and-true, old-fashioned precepts. The weight is a shade forward. With my line decided on, I work on getting the right speed. I try to take the putter back with both hands, directly on the line. I try to hit the ball solidly, square. I let the club head go right toward the hole.

When I fall into a spell of below-standard putting, it is generally because I am picking the putter up on the backswing and throwing my timing and my stroke off. When I check my grip at these times, I am almost certain to find that I have let my left hand slide off to the left. Turning the left hand more on top, where it should be, helps me to get back on the right path.

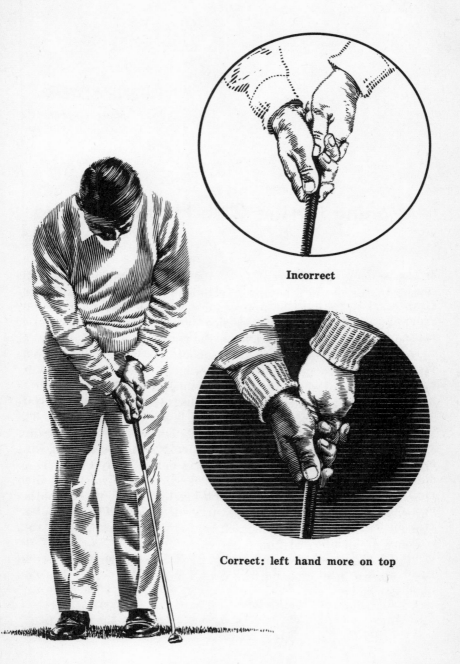

Incorrect

Correct: left hand more on top

108

GENE LITTLER

San Diego, Calif.

Waiting for the Club Head in Putting

Good putting, no different from the other shots in golf, is the result of the player's having a technically correct stroke and the confidence in that stroke to execute it without "second-guessing" it. Many golfers putt with a nice even stroke on the practice green; but when they get out on the course and are fighting for a score, they become so anxious about missing a holeable putt that they try to get the ball into the cup by some "quicker" means. More often than not they miss a good percentage of these jabbed and pushed putts, because consistently accurate putting, like the longer shots in golf, is a matter of timing. The hands and the club head must work in harmonious coordination.

You must learn to wait for the club head before stroking through the ball. Most erratic putters don't. Many of them—as pictured at the right—rush the stroke in such a way that their hands are well in front of the club head at the contact. Another breed—pictured in the center—hurry the club head in such a way that their hands are lagging well behind the contact. Their stroke is sort of an upward flip.

Try to develop the confidence to play the slow rhythmic stroke you admire in a good putter. Wait for the club head. The hole will not move.

Hands too far in front

Correct

Hands too far behind

225

109

ART WALL, JR.
Masters Champion, 1959

Following Through in Putting

Putting is the most imprecise science in all of golf; and there are almost as many putting techniques as there are golfers. A technique I have found successful is to try to think of throwing my right palm out and into the hole. This helps me keep the putter blade square to the hole and prevents pulling or pushing the putt off line.

Successful putting is largely in the mind, anyway, and I find it helps give me the right mental image, the right feel, if I rest the putter shaft against the fleshy heel of my right palm. My left hand leads just slightly in the stroke, but when I have made a good putt, I feel the sense of the hit in that right palm.

I stand with my right elbow just barely touching my right hip—not resting on it, just brushing it. Then, if I concentrate on aiming my right palm for the hole, I usually find that I stroke the kind of putt I want. It seems to me that concentration, which is the absolute core of good putting, is made easier if the golfer focuses his attention on one detail only, whether it is this one or one of his own choosing.

Shaft rests against
heel of right hand

Art Wall throws
his right palm
"into" the hole

227

110

ARNOLD BROWNING

Guyan Golf and Country Club, Huntington, W. Va.

Reading the Grain of the Green

Since thirty to forty-five per cent of your total strokes are putts, whatever would improve your putting is worth your thought and study. An important part of putting understood by few average golfers is how to read the grain or the directional "nap" of a green.

Generally, the grass on any one green will be consistent in the direction of its growth. On some mountain and seaside courses the grasses on all the greens grow in the same direction. However, on most courses you will find an occasional green that is inconsistent in itself—the grass in one part of the green has an entirely different directional nap than the grass in another part of that same green. The most important place to look is around the cup, since the ball will be traveling slower there and will be more affected by the grain.

You can usually get a quick idea of the grain you're dealing with by looking at an area some ten to twenty feet from you. If it has a dark cast to it, you can figure that the grass is growing toward you. (Putting *against* the grain, you must tap the ball harder.) If the grass has a light, glossy sheen to it, you can figure that the grass is growing away from you. (Putting *with* the grain, you would naturally tap the ball a shade softer.) I think it is too complicating for the average golfer to bother unduly with crossgrains.

Against the grain

With the grain

III

KATHY CORNELIUS

Miami Valley GC, Dayton, Ohio

Putting the Long Ones

One of the less conspicuous factors in any good round of golf is sound, steady approach putting. Regularly getting the long ones up close so that the second putt is a relatively routine tap-in—this takes a lot of worry and tension off your shoulders and promotes a comfortable frame of mind.

It helps in approach putting if you think primarily in terms of getting the distance right. Since I hit my short putts with a tap stroke, I find my feeling for distance is best if I tap the long putts too. I use a little free motion going back but I do not take the club back far. On the forward stroke, I try to "dead-wrist" it after impact. This, I realize, is an odd expression and I will explain it as best I can. After impact, whatever follow-through there is comes from the momentum and weight of the clubhead itself, not from any continued through-movement by the hands and wrists. Dead-wristing the putt gives me the sense of tap I like to have.

In regard to lining up, I follow the same fundamentals on long putts as on the short ones. I rest the left elbow lightly on the left hip bone. Both toes are on the same line, and, similarly, the knees, hips and shoulders are evenly aligned. This, I believe, helps develop a uniform motion and a square blade.

230

112

DOUG FORD

Masters Champion, 1957

Tapping the Short Putt

When I have a putt of six feet or less, I make a slight change in the stance I use for longer putts. I stand so that the ball—which is off my left toe on all putts—is an inch nearer my foot.

Moving the ball in that inch changes the feeling I get about the kind of stroke needed to contact the ball squarely. My hands feel tappier. By this, I mean I get the feeling as I line myself up that I can hit the ball much more solidly and more decisively—that my stroke doesn't have to travel so far either going back or coming forward or have as much delicate timing to it. It works that way for me. It cuts down the backswing, enables me to tap the ball very firmly, and I find that the tap action automatically makes me follow through without my having to really think about following through.

When a player taps the ball in a crisp manner, he is bound to get the ball started right, and the most important part of any putt is the first six or eight inches. If the ball is rolling right then, it will roll right all the way.

233

113

MIKE SOUCHAK

Grossinger, N. Y.

The Crucial Four-Footer

Like all professional golfers, I have tried to work out a set of fundamental procedures for keeping my putting strokes as consistent and as reliable as I can make them. Staying with these fundamentals has helped me a good deal, particularly in holing the short ones—those crucial four-footers that make or break a golf round more than any other shot in the game.

As for my grip, I've discovered that I have a much better touch if my right hand rides high on the shaft. Besides eliminating the tendency to pull the putt, this position helps me to get a uniform speed on the ball.

As far as address goes, I find it valuable to use a slight forward press of the hands before taking the blade back. Too much of a forward press can be bad, because a golfer then tends to jab the ball down into the grass. A slight forward press makes it easier for the left hand to go through the ball after contact, to move a little more out toward the hole. This, I find, enables you to get the slow speed on the ball that's so desirable. As for my right hand, I like to feel that the right palm is moving straight along the line of the putt to the hole.

The slight forward
press at address

The left hand contin-
ues through the ball

235